the Gluten-free
kitchen

the Gluten-free kitchen

Over 100 simple, irresistible recipes that everyone will enjoy.

METRO BOOKS
New York

CONTENTS

INTRODUCTION 7

RECIPE AND INGREDIENT INFORMATION 9

UNDERSTANDING CELIAC DISEASE 10

PARTY FOOD 12

SOUPS AND LIGHT COURSES 38

ENTRÉES 64

SIDE DISHES 126

SWEET FOOD 170

SAUCES AND BASICS 192

COOK'S TIPS 210

UTENSILS 215

ACKNOWLEDGEMENTS 221

INTRODUCTION

I cannot believe that I am writing the introduction to my second gluten-free cookbook. Many years after being diagnosed with celiac disease, I ventured into writing *Sharing Sweet Secrets: Gluten & Wheat Free* because I craved desserts and sweet treats that tasted "normal". Having satisfied my sweet tooth, I decided to write *The Gluten-free Kitchen*. This book is about cooking gluten-free food with a dash of panache.

I was diagnosed with celiac disease over 23 years ago. The diagnosis took about 18 months and by that time I was malnourished and anemic, weighing just 77 pounds. I was extremely ill, but within two weeks of eating gluten-free food, my health began to improve. I'd forgotten how wonderful it was to be well. I embraced the gluten-free diet because I felt so lucky to be able to manage celiac disease by diet and not medication. I began to think about what food I could eat and enjoy, not about what I might be missing out on. It was not long before I realised that a gluten-free diet was the key to good health and wellbeing for people with celiac disease or non-celiac gluten intolerance.

Cooking, eating, reading about food, "talking" food, and creating recipes are what I do. This book contains mostly savory food recipes with a small section on sweet food. They are recipes that I cook for family and friends and range from everyday quick and easy to entertaining with style. No one will ever realise that some ingredients are slightly different, as the end result is not only appealing to the eye, but full of flavor as well. Cooking gluten-free food is no more challenging than "normal" cooking. You will be able to relax and enjoy yourself knowing that the food you have prepared will be safe and delicious for everyone.

Many of my recipes can be prepared in advance and finished with a minimum of fuss. There are chapters on party food, soup and light courses, entrées, side dishes, sweet food, and sauces and basics. I have included serving suggestions for the entrées. You will also find savory or sweet secrets that I share with you. These may include how to vary the recipe, substitute ingredients, information about a particular ingredient, or an additional recipe suggestion. I hope you will find my cook's tips interesting and helpful too.

I'm amazed (and pleased) at how much things have changed since I was first diagnosed with celiac disease. There were so few gluten-free products available and most were inedible. Food manufacturers have finally realised that there is a boom going on in gluten-free food. We are now spoiled for choice as most supermarkets and health-food stores are stocking a large range of gluten-free flours, including arrowroot, amaranth, brown and white rice, besan (chickpea flour), buckwheat, chestnut, soy, potato, tapioca, pure maize, and quinoa. Manufactured gluten-free all-purpose and self-rising flours are also readily available.

Celiacs enjoy one of the healthiest diets around, with emphasis placed on eating fresh, natural food. Many of my recipes are naturally gluten free but where you see **GF** next to manufactured products in the listed ingredients, it means to look for the gluten-free equivalent. Foods that are naturally free from gluten include fish, meat, poultry, fats and oils, legumes, rice, millet, quinoa, fresh fruit and vegetables, herbs, nuts, eggs, milk and natural yogurt (note: flavored milk and flavored yogurt may contain gluten). Noodles and pasta made from rice, corn, and buckwheat, as well as polenta, which is one of my favourites, are all gluten free. Tea, coffee, most spirits, and wine are also gluten free. We can even buy gluten-free beer now! One of my recipes for a light and crisp batter contains one of these gluten-free beers. What a treat for those of us with celiac disease who cannot eat store-bought fish and chips!

Where to begin? I find it helps to have a pantry well stocked with gluten-free ingredients. Having the basics on hand makes gluten-free cooking easy. My "must haves" include gluten-free flours, pasta, noodles, rice, millet, quinoa, legumes, tins of tomatoes, gluten-free concentrated tomato purée, fish sauce, soy sauce, tamari, Worcestershire sauce, vinegars, chutneys, and mustards. I like to have different types of oils, including olive, vegetable, canola, grape seed, bran, and sesame. I keep a good supply of nuts and dried fruit in my pantry too. Essentials in my refrigerator are butter, free-range eggs, milk, cream, ricotta, yogurt and cheese. I always look for quality and flavor when purchasing seasonal fruit and vegetables.

One of our staples of course, is gluten-free bread. I've often heard people complain about the taste of it but I think the quality has improved so much over the years, and where would we be without it? I keep loaves frozen and always have gluten-free bread crumbs in the freezer. I use them in stuffing mixtures, sweet and savory crumbles, and in tortes. I like to make my own broths too because they are far superior in flavor and nutrition to any store-bought bouillon cubes. I freeze broth in portions ready to use in soup, sauces, and risotto. Like most people, I do occasionally resort to gluten-free bouillon cubes for convenience (as you will see in my recipes) but generally speaking, nothing beats a good home-made broth. The listed ingredients in all of my recipes are readily available in supermarkets, health-food and speciality stores.

I hope you will find the ideas and easy-to-follow recipes in *The Gluten-free Kitchen* imaginative and inspirational. You will be able to cook delicious food with that dash of panache suitable for any occasion, whether for a cocktail party, brunch, lunch or dinner.

Happy cooking and dining!

RECIPE AND INGREDIENT INFORMATION

Measurements

All spoon and cup measurements are level unless stated to the contrary in a recipe.

Oven temperatures

For fan-forced ovens, as a general rule you will need to set the oven temperature 35°F lower than indicated in the recipe.

Ingredients

When choosing ingredients, always read the labels carefully as companies do change their product ingredients from time to time. Keep in mind that there are many products that are naturally gluten free, but it is always wise to check ingredients listed on labels.

Where you see **GF** (meaning gluten-free) in bold capital letters next to certain manufactured products in the listed ingredients, it means to look for the gluten-free equivalent in the supermarket, health-food, or speciality store.

Those who might be at risk from the effects of salmonella poisoning (the elderly, pregnant women, young children, and anyone with immune-deficiency diseases) should consult their doctor with any concerns about eating raw eggs, as for example, in my whole-egg mayonnaise recipe.

I mostly use fresh herbs when cooking so unless I have specified "dried", fresh is best. The same goes for citrus juices (lemon, lime, orange, etc.). Where juice is used in a recipe, I always use freshly squeezed.

UNDERSTANDING CELIAC DISEASE—A BRIEF EXPLANATION

Celiac disease (pronounced seel-ee-ack) is an autoimmune disease. This means the body mistakenly produces antibodies that damage its own tissues. Celiac disease is a permanent intestinal intolerance to dietary gluten found in barley, wheat, oats, and rye. A number of serious health consequences can result if the condition is not diagnosed and treated properly. In those with untreated celiac disease, the mucosa (lining) of the small bowel (small intestine) is damaged: the tiny, finger-like projections that line the bowel (villi) become flattened and inflamed. The function of this mucosa is to break down and absorb nutrients in food.

Symptoms

The symptoms of celiac disease reflect the consequences of chronic malabsorption and may include the following:
* severe diarrhea, rumbling stomach, flatulence, stomach distension, constipation, bloating, and cramping
* nausea and vomiting
* fatigue, weakness, lethargy, tiredness, and irritability
* anemia—an iron or folic acid deficiency is common
* recurrent mouth ulcers and/or swelling of mouth or tongue
* bone and joint pain
* weight loss—although many people do not lose weight and some can even gain weight.

Who gets celiac disease and how is it diagnosed?

People are born with a genetic predisposition to developing celiac disease. They inherit a particular genetic make-up (HLA type) with the genes DQ2 and DQ8 being identified as the "celiac genes". Gene testing is presently available through pathology laboratories (by blood test or oral swab). The gene test is useful for excluding celiac disease. "At risk" groups include first-degree relatives of a person with celiac disease and those with type 1 diabetes or other autoimmune conditions. People belonging to these groups should be screened for celiac disease.

Celiac blood tests are used for initial screening ("celiac serology and IgA"). If the results are positive, further testing is warranted. A gastroenterologist will perform a gastroscopy (an endoscope is passed through the mouth into the small bowel) to collect tiny samples (biopsies) from the small bowel. The biopsy is examined under a microscope to determine if celiac disease is present. A second biopsy is usually performed after 12 months on a gluten-free diet to show that bowel repair has occurred.

Treatment

Strict adherence to a gluten-free diet for life is the only treatment for celiac disease.

Note

This is not a medical book. The above information should be used as a guide only. If you are unwell and suspect celiac disease, seek professional advice from a qualified medical practitioner.

PARTY FOOD

chickpea flat bread . . . 14

chorizo parsley puffs . . . 16

roasted beet dip . . . 18

spicy sweet potato dip . . . 18

éclairs with smoked salmon & horseradish cream . . . 20

grilled oysters with spinach & pine nuts . . . 22

polenta pizza bites . . . 24

seeded Parmesan wafers . . . 26

smoked salmon pinwheels . . . 28

smoked salmon rosti rolls . . . 30

stuffed black grapes . . . 32

thai chicken patties on cucumber . . . 34

white corn tortilla melts . . . 36

chickpea flat bread

Besan is roasted chickpea flour and has a creamy color. These flat breads are nutritious and tasty; I can never resist eating the first one straight out of the pan! They are very satisfying and can be eaten a number of ways. See "Savory secrets" for variations.

MAKES 5 FLAT BREADS

1 cup besan (chickpea flour)

2½ tablespoons olive oil

zest of 1 lemon, finely grated

2 teaspoons sumac* (optional)

bran oil, for frying

place besan in a food processor. Combine 1 cup water and olive oil in a small pitcher. With the motor running, slowly pour the mixture through the feed tube. Scrape down the sides of the bowl.

add zest, sumac, if using, and salt, to taste. Process again. Transfer batter to a pitcher so that it is easy to pour.

heat a 9½ inch nonstick crepe pan over medium–high heat. Add 1 teaspoon of bran oil and pour in one-fifth of the batter. Tilt and swirl pan so batter covers the base.

cook until bread sets on top and browns lightly on the bottom. This will take about 1 minute. Turn to cook other side. Slide flat bread onto a wire rack.

stir batter between making each flat bread. Thin batter with a little water if necessary. Add 1 teaspoon of bran oil to the pan before making each flat bread. Continue until you have used all of the batter.

SAVORY SECRETS

Sumac* is a lemony spice available from some supermarkets and Middle Eastern grocery stores.

This is a very versatile recipe. Use the flat bread as you would a wrap or savory crepe. Cut in wedges to serve with dips or tapenade and soft goat curd.

To make **chunky chickpea & scallion flat bread** prepare batter (as above), add 2 thinly sliced scallions, ½ cup drained and rinsed canned chickpeas and 2 teaspoons ground cumin. Process batter briefly so that it retains some texture from the chickpeas. Thin chickpea batter with a little water if necessary. You can freeze remaining chickpeas from the can or use them in another recipe.

To make **seeded chickpea flat bread** prepare batter (as above), add 2 teaspoons sesame seeds and 1 teaspoon each poppy seeds and nigella seeds.

Chickpea flat bread may be frozen. Layer cooked flat bread with freezer wrap and place in a zip-lock bag or wrap in foil. For a soft texture, reheat flat bread in a microwave on high for 10 seconds or under the broiler for crisp flat bread.

chorizo parsley puffs

Prepare the chorizo parsley mixture before you make the fail-proof choux pastry.

MAKES APPROXIMATELY 30

3 ounces **GF** chorizo sausage, thinly sliced

2 tablespoons roughly chopped flat-leaf (Italian) parsley

1 quantity **fail-proof choux pastry** (page 206)

line two baking sheets with parchment paper.

preheat oven to 400°F.

heat a small skillet over medium heat. Add chorizo and cook until lightly browned (there is no need to add oil to the pan). Drain on kitchen paper.

place chorizo in a food processor and pulse to crumble. Combine with parsley, transfer to a bowl, and set aside.

wipe processor bowl with kitchen paper.

prepare choux pastry.

add reserved chorizo and parsley mixture to the choux pastry and pulse to combine or fold in by hand.

place mounds of mixture, 2 teaspoons at a time, 2 inches apart on the prepared baking sheets.

bake choux for 20–25 minutes until puffed and golden. Place on a wire rack to cool.

SAVORY SECRETS
The puffs may be baked in advance and reheated in the oven until crisp to serve. They may also be frozen.

Substitute **GF** bacon for the **GF** chorizo.

To make **vegetarian puffs** replace **GF** chorizo with 2 tablespoons chopped semi-dried tomatoes, 1 or 2 tablespoons drained, rinsed, and chopped capers, 1 tablespoon chopped pitted olives, and 2 tablespoons chopped flat-leaf (Italian) parsley. Combine with choux pastry and bake as above.

dips

roasted beet dip

My daughter Kate contributed this recipe. She suggests baking extra beets and using the remainder in a salad or serving them as a warm vegetable with crème fraîche.

MAKES ABOUT 1 CUP

3 medium beets, rinsed well

2 teaspoons olive oil, plus extra, to brush

½ cup **GF** Greek-style yogurt

½ teaspoon garam masala

½ teaspoon ground cumin

½ teaspoon ground coriander

2 teaspoons lemon juice

½ teaspoon roasted cumin seeds, to finish

preheat oven to 350°F.

place beets on a sheet of foil, brush with extra olive oil, and wrap in the foil. Place on a baking sheet and bake for 1 hour or until tender when pierced with a skewer. Cool beets and, wearing latex gloves, peel.

chop beets roughly and place in a food processor. Add 2 teaspoons olive oil, yogurt, spices, and lemon juice. Season with salt and freshly ground black pepper and process until smooth. Spoon dip into a bowl and sprinkle with roasted cumin seeds.

serve with **chickpea flat breads** (page 14) or **GF** crackers.

SAVORY SECRET
To make **quick yogurt dip** add 1–2 teaspoons harissa paste to 1 cup **GF** Greek-style yogurt. Add freshly chopped cilantro leaves, to finish.

spicy sweet potato dip

MAKES ABOUT 2 CUPS

1 tablespoon unsalted butter, melted

1 garlic clove, crushed

2¼ cups peeled and cubed sweet potato

½ teaspoon sweet smoked paprika, plus extra, to finish

1 teaspoon olive oil, plus extra, to drizzle

2 scallions, finely chopped

1½ inch piece fresh ginger, grated

1 fresh red chile, seeded and finely chopped, to taste

½ cup canned butterbeans (lima beans), drained and rinsed

zest and juice of 1 lemon or lime

line a baking sheet with parchment paper.

preheat oven to 350°F.

combine butter and garlic, brush all over sweet potato, and sprinkle with paprika. Place on prepared baking sheet and bake for 25 minutes or until tender.

heat a small skillet over medium heat. Add olive oil and any remaining garlic butter to the pan. Add scallions, ginger, and chile and sauté until the mixture has softened.

transfer sweet potato and the scallion mixture to a food processor. Whizz to purée, scraping down sides of the processor. Add butterbeans, zest, and juice and purée until smooth. Transfer dip to a bowl, drizzle with olive oil, and sprinkle with paprika.

serve with **chickpea flat breads** (page 14) or **GF** crackers.

éclairs with smoked salmon & horseradish cream

These wonderful little éclairs never fail to please. They are the perfect finger food as they can be prepared several weeks in advance, frozen, then simply thawed and filled several hours before your guests arrive.

MAKES APPROXIMATELY 24

éclairs

1 quantity **fail-proof choux pastry** (page 206)

horseradish cream

heaping ¾ cup cream cheese, cut into small cubes

2 tablespoons **GF** prepared horseradish

zest of 1 lemon, finely grated

1 tablespoon finely chopped flat-leaf (Italian) parsley or dill (optional)

additional ingredients

6 smoked salmon slices, each cut into 4 slices

line two baking sheets with parchment paper.

preheat oven to 400°F.

for the éclairs

fit icing bag with a ⅝ inch nozzle and pipe éclairs 2 inches in length onto prepared baking sheets.

bake for 20–25 minutes until puffed, crisp, and golden brown. Allow to cool on a wire rack.

for the horseradish cream

prepare horseradish cream using a food processor. With the motor running, drop cream cheese cubes, one at a time, through the feed tube. Add horseradish, zest, herbs, if using, and season with freshly ground black pepper. Process well to combine.

fit icing bag with a ½ inch nozzle and fill with horseradish cream.

to finish éclairs

cut along the length of each éclair but not all the way through.

place a piece of salmon in the base of each éclair. The salmon should hang over the sides a little.

pipe horseradish cream along the length of salmon.

fold top of éclair over horseradish cream, leaving a little cream exposed.

SAVORY SECRETS

Fill éclairs or choux puffs with alternative fillings, for example rare roast beef with horseradish cream made as above, substituting crème fraîche for cream cheese. Soft goat curd topped with caramelized onions is another option. If you choose either of these fillings, use a spoon instead of a icing bag to fill the éclairs or puffs.

grilled oysters with spinach & pine nuts

Oysters, you either love them or not. I'm a fan and often serve them with drinks. When serving, offer a small fork to your guests to dislodge the oyster from the shell. You can also serve the oysters as a starter.

MAKES 24

24 oysters on the half-shell, rinsed quickly if gritty, excess water removed

topping

⅓ cup day-old **GF** bread crumbs*

4 tablespoons unsalted butter, softened

10 spinach leaves, blanched, drained on kitchen paper, and finely chopped

2 tablespoons grated Parmesan cheese

2 tablespoons chopped flat-leaf (Italian) parsley

1 tablespoon snipped chives

1 tablespoon pine nuts

zest of 1 lemon, finely grated

line a baking sheet with rock salt or crumpled foil.

preheat broiler to high.

sit oysters on top of salt or foil on the baking sheet. This will hold oysters steady.

place bread crumbs in a bowl and use your fingers to rub in the butter. Add remaining ingredients and combine well.

spoon mixture on top of oysters.

broil for 2–3 minutes or until topping is golden.

serve immediately.

SAVORY SECRETS

GF bread crumbs* see **cook's tips—bread** (page 210).

Topping may be prepared several hours in advance. Cover and refrigerate until required. Spoon topping on top of oysters just before grilling.

To make **ashed brie & almond oysters** place very thin slices of ashed brie on top of oysters and scatter with slivered almond or pine nuts. Broil oysters for several minutes until brie melts and nuts turn golden brown. Ashed brie is available in the cheese or deli section of most supermarkets. For a special occasion, stand the broiled oysters in shot glasses to serve. Place a tiny piece of removable adhesive under each shot glass to anchor it to a platter.

polenta pizza bites

You can make one large pizza instead of pizza bites. See "Savory secret" below.

MAKES APPROXIMATELY 40 PIECES

3 cups **GF** chicken or **GF** vegetable broth (I use a **GF** bouillon cube for this recipe) or water instead of broth

½ cup coarse polenta

½ cup fine (one-minute) polenta

2 tablespoons chopped flat-leaf (Italian) parsley (optional)

2–3 tablespoons olive oil

1 garlic clove, crushed

GF concentrated tomato purée or other bottled **GF** puréed tomatoes to spread on pizza bases

toppings

GF bacon or **GF** salami, red peppers, pitted black olives, Parmesan cheese, and oregano.

Prosciutto, **GF** bacon or **GF** salami, preserved artichoke hearts, flat-leaf (Italian) parsley, and grated Parmesan cheese.

Roasted diced winter squash, crumbled feta, sliced pitted black olives, and dusted with sweet paprika.

Mozzarella or bocconcini, semi-dried tomatoes or fresh cherry tomatoes, basil, and a good grinding of black pepper.

Chargrilled and finely chopped vegetables including eggplant, red pepper, and zucchini, topped with grated Parmesan cheese and sprinkled with oregano.

line a 12 x 10 inch baking pan or dish with parchment paper, then line a baking sheet with parchment paper.

preheat oven to 350°F.

place broth or salt and water in a heavy-based saucepan over high heat and bring to a boil.

mix coarse and fine polenta together and pour into the boiling water in a thin, steady stream. Stir constantly with a wooden spoon.

reduce heat to a slow steady simmer and stir until polenta thickens. This takes about 3 minutes. When cooked a wooden spoon should stand upright in the polenta. Stir in parsley, if using.

spoon polenta into prepared baking pan and flatten with dampened hands or a spatula. To avoid burning your hands wear latex gloves. Cool polenta, cover with plastic wrap, and refrigerate until firm.

turn polenta out of dish onto a flat surface and cut into small pieces measuring approximately 2 x 1 inches.

combine oil and garlic and brush one side of each piece of polenta lightly with oil. Place oiled side down on prepared baking sheet. Spread a little concentrated tomato purée on polenta pieces and add topping of your choice. Bake polenta pizza bites for about 15–20 minutes or until cheese is lightly browned.

SAVORY SECRET

To prepare a large pizza on a parchment-paper-lined pizza tray, brush the parchment paper with garlic-flavored oil before flattening polenta on the tray. Spread base with **GF** concentrated tomato purée or puréed tomatoes and toppings of your choice. Bake as above.

seeded Parmesan wafers

These crunchy crisp wafers are very easy to put together and are ever so more-ish. You can also try other seeds including mustard, cumin, and caraway. Enjoy wafers with drinks or soup.

MAKES APPROXIMATELY 20

1 cup finely grated Parmesan cheese

2 teaspoons coarse polenta

2 teaspoons pure maize cornstarch

2 teaspoons white rice flour

1½ teaspoons nigella seeds*

1 teaspoon poppy seeds

1 teaspoon sesame seeds

2 teaspoons olive oil

1 large egg, white only

line two baking sheets with parchment paper.

preheat oven to 325°F.

place Parmesan, polenta, cornstarch, rice flour, and seeds in a bowl. Stir to combine. Add olive oil and egg white. Using your fingers, bring the mixture together to make a dough.

place dough between two sheets of parchment paper, flatten it a little, then using a rolling pin, roll the dough out thinly. Refrigerate for 15 minutes. Remove top sheet of parchment paper and cut dough into irregular shapes with a knife or use pastry cutters to shape. Place wafers on prepared baking sheets. Reshape if necessary.

bake for 10–12 minutes until golden, swapping baking sheets halfway through cooking time. Leave to cool on trays for a few minutes before removing to a wire rack to cool completely.

store in an airtight container for 1 week.

SAVORY SECRETS
Nigella seeds* are available from health-food and speciality stores. They are jet black in color, have an aromatic, smoky flavor, and are popular in Middle Eastern and Indian cookery.

smoked salmon pinwheels

These pinwheels look very elegant and taste fabulous.

8 smoked salmon slices

cream cheese filling

½ cup cream cheese, cut into small cubes

1 tablespoon finely chopped preserved lemon* peel (rinse the preserved lemon first, discard the pulp, and use only the peel)

2 teaspoons lemon juice

1 tablespoon chopped flat-leaf (Italian) parsley or snipped chives

additional ingredients

2 tablespoons capers, rinsed well if salted and drained on kitchen paper

2–3 small cucumbers

place a sheet of freezer wrap measuring 16 x 6 inches on a flat surface. Form a rectangle with the salmon slices by placing them side by side (one up, one down) on the freezer wrap. Cut salmon to fill in gaps if necessary. You should now have a rectangle of salmon measuring approximately 12 x 3½ inches.

prepare the cream cheese filling in a food processor. With the motor running, drop cubes of cream cheese, one at a time, through the feed tube. Add preserved lemon, lemon juice, and parsley.

spread a thin coating of cream cheese filling over the salmon. Add a little extra lemon juice if cream cheese filling is too firm to spread. Sprinkle with capers.

roll the salmon into a long roll using the freezer wrap as a guide. Place in the refrigerator to firm. The roll can be prepared a day in advance.

peel cucumbers but leave some thin green strips. Score lengthways with a fork and cut into ¼ inch rounds. Place rounds on kitchen paper and cover with more kitchen paper to remove excess moisture.

cut roll into pinwheels approximately ½ inch thick using a very sharp thin-bladed knife. Place pinwheels on cucumber. Wipe blade between cuts.

SAVORY SECRETS

Preserved lemon* is available in supermarkets or prepare **preserved lemons** (page 202).

Cucumber may be prepared several hours in advance. Leave it to rest on kitchen paper in refrigerator until required. Place salmon pinwheels on cucumber just before serving.

Substitute **GF** crackers for the cucumber rounds.

smoked salmon rosti rolls

The taste and texture of these rolls is sublime! You'll keep on coming back for more.

MAKES 20–24

potato rosti

2 cups peeled and coarsely grated all-purpose potatoes, such as Desiree or Sebago

3 scallions, finely chopped, or snipped chives

1 tablespoon baby capers, rinsed well if salted and drained on kitchen paper

additional ingredients

unsalted butter and bran oil for cooking the rosti

8 smoked salmon slices, cut into rectangles approximately 4 x 1 inch

¼ cup **GF** prepared horseradish or **wasabi mayonnaise** (page 61)

line a bowl with several layers of kitchen paper. Place grated potato on top and cover with more kitchen paper. Press down firmly to remove excess moisture and leave to drain for several minutes.

discard kitchen paper and reserve grated potato in the bowl.

combine scallions and capers with potato.

heat about 1 teaspoon each of butter and oil in a small nonstick skillet.

place 5 or 6 small mounds (about 2 teaspoons each) of rosti mixture in the pan and fry over medium heat until golden and crisp on both sides. Drain on kitchen paper and set aside.

wipe skillet with kitchen paper before making more rosti. Add another teaspoon each butter and oil. Cook rosti until you have used all the mixture.

spread each rectangle of salmon with prepared horseradish. Place a rosti on the salmon and roll up.

serving suggestion

To "stand" the rosti rolls upright on a platter, place a salmon rosti roll upright on a work surface and push the base down gently but firmly. Place on platter and repeat with remaining rolls.

SAVORY SECRETS

To vary the potato rosti add lemon zest and parsley to the mixture before frying.

To prepare potato rosti in advance, place the cooked rosti on a foil-lined baking sheet. When you are ready to serve the rosti, pop them under the broiler to crisp. Be sure to watch the rosti as they will only take a minute to crisp. Cut smoked salmon into rectangles, place on a plate or tray, spread with prepared horseradish, cover, and place in the refrigerator until you are ready to roll the rosti.

Prepare larger potato rosti to serve with broiled or pan-fried fish, chicken, beef, or lamb.

Purée any pieces of leftover salmon with cream cheese, lemon juice, and chives to make a spread or dip. Alternatively, fold smoked salmon pieces through scrambled eggs to serve for breakfast.

stuffed black grapes

These grapes have to be one of my favorite finger foods as they not only taste superb, but can be prepared well in advance. They are perfect nibbles to have with a glass of Champagne.

MAKES 36

36 large black globe grapes

filling

scant ½ cup cream cheese, softened

scant ½ cup chèvre*, soft but firm, similar in texture to cream cheese

1 scallion, white part only, very finely chopped

finely grated zest of 1 lime

1 teaspoon lime juice

additional ingredients

½ cup finely chopped toasted almonds, hazelnuts, or walnuts

blend ingredients for the filling with some freshly ground black pepper in a food processor.

use a small sharp knife to cut the grapes in half lengthways to the center, but do not cut all the way through. Remove seeds with a small teaspoon. Drain grapes on kitchen paper.

place a small teaspoon of the filling in each grape crevice. Gently close grape , leaving some of the cream cheese mixture exposed.

roll each filled grape, cream cheese side only, in nuts and place on a platter. Refrigerate until required.

SAVORY SECRETS
Chèvre* is cheese made from goat milk. You can use cream cheese only if you wish but the chèvre adds a little something.

thai chicken patties on cucumber

These little morsels can be prepared well in advance and taste great cold. Larger patties can be prepared for a delicious main course.

MAKES APPROXIMATELY
20 PATTIES

thai chicken patties

9 ounces skinless, boneless chicken breast, roughly diced

2 scallions, sliced

1 garlic clove, crushed

1 tablespoon chopped cilantro leaves and stems

1 tablespoon chopped mint

3 teaspoons **GF** fish sauce

2 teaspoons grated fresh ginger

1 pinch of sugar

¼ teaspoon chile paste or 1 red chile, seeded and finely chopped, to taste

3 teaspoons potato flour

additional ingredients

peanut or bran oil for shallow-frying

2–3 small cucumbers, peeled and cut into ¼ inch rounds

cilantro leaves, to finish

GF sweet chile sauce, to finish

place chicken in a food processor and whizz to grind. Remove from processor and set aside.

place remaining patty ingredients and some freshly ground black pepper in the processor and process to a paste. Add ground chicken and pulse to combine.

form mixture into even walnut-sized balls and then flatten to make small patties. Wet hands with water before forming the mixture into balls.

shallow pan-fry patties in oil. Drain on kitchen paper.

place patties on cucumber rounds and place a tiny amount of sweet chile sauce on top. Garnish with a cilantro leaf.

SAVORY SECRETS

Substitute white-fleshed fish or pork filet for the chicken.

To vary the recipe, add some drained and chopped water chestnuts to the patty mixture. You can also dip the patties in dried rice flakes before frying. Rice flakes are available from Asian grocery stores.

Prepare patties in advance. Freeze mixture raw. Thaw and cook on the day they are to be eaten.

Make larger patties for a main course. Serve with **GF** vermicelli noodles, shredded carrot, thinly sliced cucumber, and chopped roasted peanuts. Serve in a butter leaf lettuce cup and top with a **GF** Asian dipping sauce or **GF** sweet chile sauce.

white corn tortilla melts

Quesadillas is the correct name for these melts. I often make them for lunch as they are quick and delicious. If you are serving melts with drinks, omit the jalapeño, if you wish.

MAKES 12 QUARTERS OR 24 SMALLER
WEDGES TO HAVE WITH DRINKS

filling

1 cup grated Cheddar cheese

6 **GF** ham slices, diced

preserved sliced jalapeño peppers*,
to taste (optional)

2 or 3 small tomatoes, seeded and diced or semi-dried tomatoes, chopped

chopped herbs—use whatever you have available, such as parsley, cilantro, or basil

additional ingredients

6 white corn tortillas**

bran oil, for shallow-frying

combine filling ingredients in a bowl.

brush one side of a tortilla generously with oil and place oiled side down on a flat surface. Spread one-third of the filling over the tortilla. Place another tortilla on top, brush with oil, and set aside. Repeat with remaining tortillas. You should have three double-sided tortillas to fry.

heat a nonstick skillet over medium–high heat. Carefully lift a prepared tortilla into the pan and fry for several minutes until golden brown. Slide tortilla onto a plate, cover with skillet, and invert back into the pan to cook the other side. Repeat with remaining tortillas.

serve cut into wedges.

serving suggestion
They are great served with **guacamole salsa** (page 146).

SAVORY SECRETS
Preserved sliced jalapeño peppers* and white corn tortillas** are available in some supermarkets or health food stores.

Vary the fillings—anything that you put on a pizza you can put in tortillas. You need to add cheese so that the tortillas hold together when fried.

For a strong cheesy taste, mix grated Parmesan with Cheddar

SOUPS AND LIGHT COURSES

soups

asian rice congee . . . 40

cauliflower soup with cumin & Parmesan croutons . . . 42

sunchoke soup with seared scallops . . . 44

peasant soup . . . 46

simple borscht with sour cream & cucumber . . . 48

summer consommé . . . 50

light courses

asian-style omelet with vermicelli & ponzu sauce . . . 52

market mushrooms with garlic bread fingers . . . 54

pizza with a dash of panache . . . 56

preserved lemon panna cotta with smoked ocean trout . . . 58

smoked salmon on toast with wasabi mayonnaise . . . 60

spanish-style omelet with potato, red pepper, & chorizo . . . 62

asian rice congee

Rice congee or "jook" is a classic Chinese breakfast dish that I love to eat for lunch and dinner too. It's a great pick-me-up if you're feeling the need for comfort food. There are no rules about what accompaniments can be add to the congee so use my suggestions as a guide only.

SERVES 8

1 cup white short-grain rice, rinsed well and drained

10 cups hot water or GF chicken broth (GF bouillon cubes are fine for this recipe)

1 teaspoon salt

2–3 inch piece fresh ginger, peeled and grated

3 garlic cloves, crushed

5 makrut (kaffir lime) leaves

2 lemon grass stems, bruised (optional)

1 fresh red chile, seeded and finely chopped, to taste

accompaniments

Poached shrimp, squid, or boneless, skinless chicken breasts, cooked pork or duck, thin omelet cut into strips, blanched or steamed vegetables, crisp-fried sliced French shallots (eschalots), scallions thinly sliced on an angle, cilantro leaves and finely chopped stems, crisp-fried fresh ginger, diced silken tofu, toasted sesame seeds, salted peanuts, finely chopped chile, sesame oil, GF fish sauce, GF soy sauce, and GF tamari.

combine all ingredients in a slow cooker (see note) and cook on high for 3 hours or on low for 6 hours. Stir about every 30 minutes during cooking time. The congee is done when the rice dissolves into a thick, creamy, porridge-like consistency. You may need to add more water/broth.

remove lime leaves and lemon grass before serving.

ladle congee into heated bowls and top with a combination of any of the accompaniments below.

note: If cooking congee in a stockpot, bring to a boil and immediately turn down to a simmer. Cook gently for about 2 hours. Stir congee occasionally to prevent sticking.

SAVORY SECRET
Poach shrimp, squid, or chicken in the congee just before serving. The chicken will take longer to poach than the prawns and squid. When chicken is cooked, slice it on an angle to serve.

cauliflower soup with cumin & Parmesan croutons

This is a winter warmer soup that is full of flavor and comfort. The croutons add texture and taste great.

cauliflower soup

¼ cup unsalted butter

1 large onion, finely chopped

1 garlic clove, crushed

1 teaspoon cumin seeds

2 bay leaves

4 cups small cauliflower florets

2 small all-purpose potatoes, peeled and diced

3 cups **GF** chicken broth

1 cup milk

⅓ cup whipping cream

cumin & Parmesan croutons

4 thick slices **GF** bread, crusts removed

2 4 tablespoons unsalted butter, melted

⅓ cup finely grated Parmesan cheese

1 teaspoon cumin seeds

lightly grease a baking sheet.

cauliflower soup

heat butter in a large saucepan or small stockpot over medium heat. Add onion and cook until softened. Add garlic and cumin seeds and cook for 30 seconds, then add bay leaves, cauliflower, potato, broth, and milk. Season with salt and freshly ground black pepper. Simmer for about 1 hour or until vegetables are well softened.

purée soup with cream in a food processor until smooth.

cumin & Parmesan croutons

brush both sides of bread with butter and cut into ⅝ inch cubes.

combine Parmesan and cumin seeds in a large bowl. Add bread cubes and toss to coat. Place in a single layer on the prepared baking sheet. Sprinkle with some of the Parmesan and cumin seed mixture remaining in the bowl.

preheat a broiler to high heat and toast croutons for 2–3 minutes until golden brown. Turn croutons, sprinkle with remaining Parmesan and cumin seed mixture, and cook until golden.

serve soup in heated bowls, topped with cumin & Parmesan croutons.

sunchoke soup with seared scallops

Sunchokes are knobbly and have a delicate earthy flavor. This soup is extremely easy to prepare and may be made several days in advance. The scallops add a touch of elegance but are optional.

SERVES 4

seared scallops

¼ cup olive oil

2 teaspoons finely chopped flat-leaf (Italian) parsley

12 scallops, cleaned, roe removed and discarded, and scallops drained on kitchen paper

soup

juice of 1 lemon

12 ounces sunchokes

2 medium all-purpose potatoes, such as Desiree

2 tablespoons unsalted butter

1 celery rib, finely chopped

1 leek, white part only, trimmed, rinsed well, and thinly sliced

2 bay leaves

1 garlic clove, crushed

3 cups **GF** chicken broth

white pepper, to taste

⅓ cup whipping cream

olive oil, to drizzle (optional)

combine olive oil and parsley in a bowl. Add scallops and turn to coat. Marinate in refrigerator for up to 2 hours. Remove from refrigerator 30 minutes before cooking.

fill a medium-sized bowl with water and add lemon juice. Peel artichokes, slice thinly, and place in lemon water. Do the same with potatoes.

melt butter in a large saucepan over medium heat. Add celery, leek, and bay leaves and cook gently for 5 minutes. Add garlic and cook briefly.

drain artichokes and potatoes very well, add to the pan, and stir for 1–2 minutes. Add stock, season well with salt and white pepper, and simmer for 35 minutes or until vegetables are soft. Remove bay leaves.

purée soup with cream in a food processor until smooth. Do this in batches. Return soup to cleaned saucepan. Reheat soup to serve.

heat a skillet over medium–high heat. Season scallops with salt and cook without disturbing for 60–90 seconds or until golden. Turn and briefly cook other side. The scallops should feel springy to touch. Drain on kitchen paper.

serve soup in heated bowls. Place three scallops on top of each bowl of soup and drizzle with olive oil, if desired, to finish.

SAVORY SECRETS
For a smoother silken-textured soup, pass the soup through a fine sieve after puréeing. Use a spoon or spatula to help push the purée through.

Substitute shrimp or lobster for the scallops.

Soup may be frozen.

peasant soup

This is one of my favorite weekend soups as it's more like a meal than a starter. Peasant soup is so thick you can almost eat it with a fork! And it's great for using up all the vegetables in your refrigerator.

SERVES 8

1 tablespoon olive oil

4 slices lean uncooked **GF** bacon, diced

1 medium onion, diced

1 medium leek, white part only, trimmed, rinsed well, and diced

2 garlic cloves, crushed

6 button or Swiss brown mushrooms, wiped over with damp kitchen paper and sliced

1 red pepper, seeded, membrane removed, diced

1 medium celery rib, diced

2 medium carrots, diced

10 green beans, trimmed and cut into small pieces, or use 1 zucchini

1 medium parsnip, diced

1 all-purpose potato, such as Desiree, peeled and diced

2 bay leaves

2 teaspoons dried oregano

2 x 14 ounce cans chopped tomatoes

1 tablespoon **GF** concentrated tomato purée

4 cups **GF** chicken or **GF** vegetable broth (you may need a little more)

14 ounce cab cannellini beans, drained and rinsed

½ cup chopped flat-leaf (Italian) parsley or a combination of herbs

Parmesan cheese, grated or shaved, to finish

heat oil in a large stockpot over medium–high heat and sauté the bacon, onion, and leek for 3 minutes. Add garlic and sauté briefly before adding remaining fresh vegetables, bay leaves, and oregano. Season with salt and freshly ground black pepper. Cook for a further 3–4 minutes.

add tomato, concentrated tomato purée, and broth and cook until vegetables are tender.

add cannellini beans and herbs and simmer for a further 10 minutes.

serve soup in heated bowls topped with Parmesan.

SAVORY SECRETS

Omit bacon to make a vegetarian soup.

To vary the soup, add 1 **GF** chorizo sausage, diced and lightly pan-fried.

You can also add 1 cup cooked rice or **GF** macaroni or small shell **GF** pasta. Pasta tends to break up if soup is reheated. I find it best to add cooked pasta just before serving.

Another ideas is to add 1 cup diced skinless chicken breast. Poach gently in the soup towards the end of cooking time.

simple borscht soup with sour cream & cucumber

This thick soup with its glorious crimson color can be eaten hot or cold.

SERVES 6

4–6 beets, trimmed and rinsed very well

1 tablespoon olive oil

1 medium onion, finely chopped

1 medium carrot, grated

1 medium celery rib, finely chopped

2 garlic cloves, crushed

14 ounce can chopped tomatoes

1 **GF** bouillon cube, chicken or vegetable flavor

1 tablespoon balsamic vinegar

¼ cup chopped fresh dill, or a combination of mint, parsley, and basil

sour cream or crème fraîche, to serve

1 small cucumber, peeled, seeded and diced

dill fronds, extra, to serve

place beets in a large saucepan and cover with approximately 4 cups water, then partially cover with a lid and cook over medium heat for 1 hour or until tender. Skim foam from cooking liquid as necessary.

strain the crimson-colored liquid using a fine sieve and reserve the liquid. Rinse saucepan.

peel beets when they have cooled. To avoid staining your hands, wear latex gloves. Grate beets coarsely and set aside.

heat oil in a saucepan over medium heat and sauté onion, carrot, celery, and garlic until softened.

add grated beets, reserved liquid, tomato, crumbled bouillon cube and vinegar and continue to cook for 5 minutes.

remove 2 cups soup and purée with a stick blender or in a food processor. Return purée to soup and stir.

add herbs and season to taste. Chill if serving soup cold.

serve with a dollop of sour cream, cucumber, and extra dill.

SAVORY SECRETS
To vary the soup, serve topped with **GF** Greek-style yogurt combined with **GF** prepared horseradish to taste.

Do not throw the beet leaves away as they are edible. Rinse well and use in salads or a stir-fry.

summer consommé

This recipe is based on chipilin consommé, a soup that my husband and I ate on Christmas Day in Antigua, Guatemala. It looks very festive and can be eaten hot or cold. I have substituted baby spinach leaves for chipilin, the leafy vegetable traditionally used in this dish.

SERVES 4

6 cups reduced **chicken broth** (see page 196)

1 cup baby English spinach leaves, cut into chiffonnade*

1 large avocado, finely diced

4 small perfectly ripe tomatoes, seeded and cut into small dice

zest of 2 limes, finely grated

1½ tablespoons lime juice

place broth in a saucepan over high heat and bring to a boil.

heat bowls if serving consommé hot and place a small mound of spinach in each bowl.

place avocado and tomato around the spinach.

add lime zest and juice to the broth just before serving.

ladle broth gently over spinach, avocado, and tomato and serve immediately.

SAVORY SECRET
The term chiffonnade* means to finely shred. To do this, stack six spinach leaves one on top of the other, roll the leaves tightly and finely slice. For this recipe, I slice through the chiffonnade lengthways so it is easy to eat.

asian-style omelet with vermicelli & ponzu sauce

At home we tend to have brunch instead of breakfast on weekends so I'm often looking for new ways to play with ingredients to keep it interesting. This recipe came about because we had leftover vermicelli noodles in the refrigerator.

SERVES 2

ponzu sauce

1 tablespoon **GF** tamari

1 tablespoon lemon or lime juice, strained

1 tablespoon fresh orange juice, strained

1 scallion, thinly sliced on an angle

¼ teaspoon **GF** wasabi paste*, or to taste

1 teaspoon light brown sugar

½ teaspoon sesame oil

1 red chile, seeded and finely chopped, to taste (optional)

omelet

⅔ cup **GF** rice vermicelli noodles

½ cup cilantro leaves, rinsed well and dried on kitchen paper

2 scallions, thinly sliced on an angle

4 large eggs

3 teaspoons fresh orange juice

1 teaspoon sesame oil

1 teaspoon bran or vegetable oil

1 tablespoon unsalted butter

whisk ingredients for the ponzu sauce together with 2 teaspoons of water in a small bowl and set aside.

place vermicelli in a bowl, cover with 3 cups boiling water, and leave for 10 minutes to soften. Use a fork to separate noodles. Drain vermicelli, spread them on a clean dish towel, and roll up to remove excess water.

combine vermicelli, cilantro leaves, and scallions in a bowl and set aside.

break eggs into a bowl, add orange juice, and whisk together.

heat oils and butter in a nonstick skillet over medium heat. Add vermicelli mixture and spread it to the edge of the pan.

pour egg mixture over and cook undisturbed for 4–5 minutes. Loosen around the edge of the omelet with a spatula. Slide omelet out of skillet onto a plate, cover with the skillet and invert omelet back into skillet. Cook for a further 2–3 minutes until done. Insert a small sharp knife into the omelet. The egg should be set, not runny.

slide omelet out of pan onto a cutting board and cut into wedges. Serve the sauce separately in small individual dishes, if you wish.

SAVORY SECRETS
Wasabi paste* is available in supermarkets and Asian grocery stores.

This omelet is delicious eaten cold. It is great to take on a picnic as you would a frittata.

Ponzu sauce can be used as a dipping sauce with other Asian-style food. It is also terrific with silken tofu, stir-fried vegetables, and noodles or fish.

market mushrooms with garlic bread fingers

It is important to use a variety of mushrooms in this recipe for both taste and texture. Dark mushrooms have more flavor than pale varieties. This is a simple starter, breakfast dish, or Sunday night dinner.

SERVES 2

market mushrooms

1 tablespoon unsalted butter

1 tablespoon olive oil

⅓ cup thinly sliced French shallots (eschalots), or use ½ a small red onion

1 garlic clove, crushed

12 ounces mixed mushrooms, including enoki, shiitake, Swiss brown and button mushrooms, wiped over with damp kitchen paper, cut in half, thick slices or wedges

zest of 1 lemon, finely grated

½ cup **GF** chicken or **GF** beef broth

2 tablespoons finely chopped flat-leaf (Italian) parsley

1 tablespoon whipping cream

garlic bread fingers

1 tablespoon olive oil

1 garlic clove, crushed

1 teaspoon finely chopped lemon thyme

4 slices **GF** bread, crusts removed and cut into 2 or 3 fingers, depending on size of bread

additional ingredients

crème fraîche or sour cream, to serve (optional)

extra chopped flat-leaf (Italian) parsley, to serve

for the market mushrooms

heat butter and oil in a large nonstick skillet over medium heat. A risotto pan also works well. Add shallots and garlic and cook until softened. Do not brown.

turn up heat and add mushrooms. Do this in several batches if necessary. Cook for about 5 minutes or until mushrooms have softened.

stir in lemon zest, broth, and parsley. Season with salt and freshly ground black pepper. Cook for 1 minute, add cream, and boil to reduce and thicken slightly. Set aside while you prepare the garlic bread fingers.

for the garlic bread fingers

preheat the broiler to high.

combine olive oil, garlic, and thyme in a small screw-top jar and shake well. Brush both sides of bread fingers and broil each side until golden.

serve market mushrooms with garlic bread fingers, a dollop of crème fraîche, if desired, and parsley.

serving suggestion
Serve with broiled or grilled steaks, soft or grilled polenta, pasta, or rice.

pizza with a dash of panache

I owe this recipe to my friend, foodie Fi. Together we created a pizza recipe that has the crisp base, light bready texture, and mouth-watering aroma of a traditional pizza.

SERVES 4

fine (one-minute) instant polenta, to sprinkle

white rice flour, for dusting

1 teaspoon sugar

1 cup warm water

5 teapoons **GF** instant dried yeast

heaping 1 cup white rice flour

½ cup potato flour

½ cup tapioca flour

½ cup gluten substitute (Orgran GfG)*

¼ cup **GF** full-fat dried milk powder

1½ teaspoons **GF** baking powder

1 teaspoon salt

1 tablespoon extra virgin olive oil

1 large egg

toppings

Blanched thinly sliced potato, sliced **GF** chorizo sausage, sliced **roasted red pepper** (page 164), mozzarella and basil pesto (page 115).

red onion & fennel confit (page 162), blanched thinly sliced winter squash, blue cheese, and served with arugula (optional).

Brush pizza base with a mixture of crushed garlic and olive oil and bake as above. Top cooked pizza with smoked salmon or ocean trout, goat curd, thinly sliced **preserved lemon** (page 202), capers, and dill. Do not bake the topping in this instance.

sprinkle baking sheets with fine (one-minute) instant polenta.

preheat oven to 200°C (400°F/Gas 6).

place sugar, ⅔ cup of the warm water, and yeast together in a small mixing bowl, stirring gently to combine. Leave to stand for 10 minutes or until the mixture becomes light and foamy and bubbles appear.

sift dry ingredients together and place in a food processor.

whisk together extra virgin olive oil and egg, then add to food processor, processing until combined. Add yeast mixture, again processing until combined. The mixture will still look rough and crumbly at this stage. To bring the mixture together, turn the food processor on and add the remaining warm water through the feed tube until the mixture comes together as a ball.

lightly dust a work surface with rice flour and gently knead the dough for 2–3 minutes until dough is no longer sticky and becomes smooth. Place dough in a lightly oiled mixing bowl, cover with plastic wrap, and leave in a warm, draft-free place until the dough has doubled in size. This will vary in time depending on the warmth of the room and may take up to 1 hour.

divide the dough into 4 or 8 even-sized pieces, depending on the pizza size you want. Use the heel of your hand to flatten and shape the dough. Place on prepared baking sheets and add toppings of your choice, leaving a ¾ inch border around the edge of the dough.

bake for 18–20 minutes or until pizza is cooked to your liking.

SAVORY SECRETS
Gluten substitute (Orgran GfG)* is available in supermarkets.

The pizza dough makes excellent **focaccia.** Once the dough has doubled in size, knock it back by gently flattening the dough and pushing some air out of it. Place the flattened dough in a large, deep, oiled cake pan and cover with plastic wrap again. Allow dough to rise again by half its size. Remove plastic wrap and press your fingertips into the dough to make indentations. Drizzle generously with olive oil and sprinkle with rosemary and sea salt. Bake in a preheated oven at 400°F for 30 minutes or until golden and crisp.

preserved lemon panna cotta with smoked ocean trout

This is a fairly rich and ever-so-sexy starter. I recommend you follow it with just a light entrée.
You can cheat with store-bought gluten-free whole-egg mayonnaise, or prepare my recipe.

SERVES 4 OR DOUBLE THE QUANTITY
FOR 6 LARGE SERVES

grape seed oil, for greasing

¼ cup milk

¼ cup whipping cream

2 teaspoons gelatine powder

2 tablespoons warm water

¼ cup **GF** Greek-style yogurt

¼ cup **GF** whole-egg mayonnaise*

1 tablespoon finely chopped preserved
lemon** peel (rinse the preserved lemon first,
discard the pulp, and use the rind only)

2 teaspoons lemon or lime juice

1 teaspoon **GF** prepared horseradish

a pinch of sweet paprika

2 small cucumbers

4–8 smoked ocean trout slices, depending
on how generous you want to be

lemon zest, thinly sliced (optional)

dill sprigs (optional)

olive oil, to drizzle (optional)

lightly grease 4 x ½ cup ramekins or dariole molds, or use Chinese teacups, with grape seed oil.

place milk and cream in a microwave-safe container and heat on high for 90 seconds. Alternatively heat in a saucepan over low heat until warm.

sprinkle gelatine over warm water and allow to soak in for 30 seconds. Microwave on medium for 30–40 seconds or until dissolved. Stir well. Alternatively, follow directions on packet to dissolve gelatine.

combine gelatine with warmed milk and cream mixture. Add yogurt and mayonnaise and stir well. Add preserved lemon, lemon juice, horseradish, and paprika and stir again to combine. Pour mixture into ramekins or dariole molds, filling each about two-thirds full. Cover with plastic wrap and place in refrigerator to set.

remove panna cotta from refrigerator 30 minutes before serving. To remove panna cotta from ramekins, run a small thin-bladed knife around the edge of the custard and invert onto plates.

slice cucumbers into long ribbons using a vegetable peeler. Try to leave an edge of green skin on some ribbons. Stop peeling when you reach the seeds. Discard the seeds.

serve panna cotta with ocean trout, a small mound of cucumber ribbons, and lemon zest. Garnish with dill.

SAVORY SECRETS

GF whole-egg mayonnaise* is available in supermarkets or prepare **whole-egg mayonnaise** (page 201).

Preserved lemons** are available in supermarkets or prepare **preserved lemons** (page 202).

Substitute smoked salmon, prawns, or lobster for the smoked ocean trout.

smoked salmon on toast with wasabi mayonnaise

Quantities for this recipe will vary according to the size of bread slices used and how generous you are with the salmon. The wasabi mayonnaise takes the place of butter.

SERVES 2

wasabi mayonnaise

½ cup **whole-egg mayonnaise** (page 201)*

2 teaspoons **GF** wasabi paste**, or to taste

finely grated zest of 2 limes

1–2 teaspoons lime juice

additional ingredients

4 slices **GF** multi-grain bread

4–8 slices smoked salmon

2 scallions, thinly sliced on an angle, to serve

thinly sliced zest of 1 lime, to finish

place mayonnaise in a bowl and add wasabi paste, zest, and juice. Stir well to blend. The mayonnaise will take on a lovely green hue. Taste and adjust if necessary.

preheat broiler to high and toast bread on both sides until golden.

place salmon on toast and spoon a dollop of wasabi mayonnaise on top. Top with scallions and lime zest, to finish.

SAVORY SECRETS

Take a short cut and purchase **GF** whole-egg mayonnaise*.

GF wasabi paste** is available in supermarkets.

To vary the recipe, add a few slices of avocado or cucumber ribbons on top of the wasabi mayonnaise and serve with a lime wedge.

Wasabi mayonnaise goes well with grilled shrimp, squid, fish, and chicken.

spanish-style omelet with potato, red pepper, & chorizo

This omelet is like a frittata and is perfect for brunch or lunch, or when baked in the oven can be cut into cubes to serve as finger food.

SERVES 4

1 pound cooked new potatoes, peeled then sliced or quartered

1 cup **roasted red capsicum** (page 164), cut into ½ inch strips, or pan-fry one large sliced red pepper

1 **GF** chorizo sausage, thinly sliced

1 teaspoon olive oil

1 medium red onion, thinly sliced

4 large eggs

¼ cup whipping cream

1 tablespoon fresh orange juice

2 tablespoons roughly chopped flat-leaf (Italian) parsley

1 teaspoon sweet smoked paprika

2 teaspoons unsalted butter

place potato and pepper in a large bowl.

heat a medium-sized nonstick skillet and cook chorizo slices until lightly browned. Drain on kitchen paper then add to potato and pepper.

add oil to pan and sauté onion over low–medium heat for about 5 minutes or until well softened. Add to large bowl and gently combine with potato, pepper, and chorizo.

place eggs, cream, orange juice, parsley, and paprika in a separate bowl and whisk to combine.

melt butter in a large nonstick skillet over medium heat. Add potato and pepper mixture and spread it to the edge of the skillet. Pour over egg mixture.

turn heat down to low. As eggs begin to set around the edge of the skillet, use a spatula to drag the cooked egg in about an inch, allowing the uncooked mixture to flow out towards the edge of the skillet. It will take about 20 minutes for the omelet to set as it is cooked gently. The omelet will still be wobbly in the center so pop it under a low–medium broiler until firm. Do not have the broiler heat too fierce or the omelet will burn. If necessary, cover skillet handle with foil to protect it from burning.

serve omelet cut into wedges.

SAVORY SECRETS

If the potato is hot when combined with pepper, chorizo, and onion, the egg mixture will begin to cook immediately, so cooking time will be less than if potato is cold or at room temperature.

The omelet can also be baked in a 9 x 9 x 2 inch) greased and baking-paper-lined ceramic ovenproof dish. Preheat oven to 325°F and bake for 20–25 minutes or until set.

ENTRÉES

fish

baked fennel & leek risotto with fish . . . 66

beer-battered fish & best potato wedges . . . 68

crunchy crusted snapper with beurre blanc . . . 70

polenta, coconut, & lime-coated fish . . . 72

sesame-glazed salmon with pickled ginger rice . . . 74

sumac fish with preserved lemon & caper salsa . . . 76

poultry & game

chicken in red wine with mushrooms & shallots . . . 78

chicken poached in ginger broth . . . 80

chicken tagine with lemon & olives . . . 82

duck breasts with saffron ginger glaze . . . 84

gremolata-stuffed chicken . . . 86

icky sticky chicken legs . . . 88

orange marmalade duck ragout . . . 90

prosciutto-wrapped chicken with leek & ricotta . . . 92

sage & citrus quail . . . 94

spatchcock with cranberry & pistachio stuffing . . . 96

spicy chicken . . . 98

beef & lamb

beef & mushroom hotpot . . . 100

chile beef with guacamole salsa . . . 102

crepe lasagne . . . 104

greek beef or lamb kabobs . . . 106

herby lamb with blue-green lentils . . . 108

italian meatloaf roll with tomato & pepper sauce . . . 110

slow-cooked lamb with raisins & pine nuts . . . 112

vegetarian

basil pesto pasta with "no-mess" poached eggs . . . 114

herbed crepes with spinach & ricotta . . . 116

mediterranean vegetable & ricotta gratin . . . 118

millet pilaf with saffron & green vegetables . . . 120

pasta with smoky sweet potato & ricotta . . . 122

red pepper & lentil potpies with feta crumble . . . 124

baked fennel & leek risotto with fish

This is a shortcut to the traditional method of making risotto on the stovetop—and equally delicious.

SERVES 4

2 teaspoons chopped fennel fronds

2 teaspoons finely grated lemon zest

3 tablespoons unsalted butter, melted

4 firm white fish filets (about 7 ounces each)

risotto

3 cups **GF** fish, **GF** chicken or **GF** vegetable broth

1 tablespoon olive oil

2 tablespoons unsalted butter

1 leek, white part only, trimmed, rinsed well, and thinly sliced

2 small fennel bulbs, trimmed and finely sliced (reserve fronds for finishing the risotto)

1 garlic clove, crushed

2 bay leaves

finely grated zest of 2 lemons

2 tablespoons lemon juice

1 cup arborio rice

½ cup dry white wine

½ cup grated Parmesan cheese

choose a large deep flameproof casserole dish or risotto pan with a lid.

preheat oven to 350°F.

combine fennel fronds, zest, and butter. Brush both sides of filets with butter mixture and place on a foil-lined baking sheet. Set aside while you cook the risotto.

place the broth in a saucepan over medium–high heat and bring to a simmer.

heat oil and butter in the casserole dish over medium–low heat and sauté leek and fennel for 3–4 minutes. Add garlic, bay leaves, and lemon zest and cook briefly. Add rice and stir for about 2 minutes, or until well coated.

add wine and boil rapidly until wine has almost evaporated. Add broth, season with salt and freshly ground black pepper, and stir to combine. Cover with lid and transfer to the oven.

bake for about 15 minutes until rice is *al dente*. Add reserved lemon juice and Parmesan, stir to combine, then cover and leave to stand while you cook the fish.

preheat broiler to high. Place fish under the broiler until just cooked through. There is no need to turn the fish if the filets are thin.

serve risotto with broiled fish and fennel fronds.

serving suggestions
Serve with baby English spinach leaves.

SAVORY SECRETS
You can replace the broiled fish with small pieces of raw fish, crabmeat, shrimp or chicken, added to the risotto towards the end of cooking time. The heat from the risotto will cook the meat. Stir in some fresh dill to serve.

For a creamy (soupy) risotto, add 2 tablespoons extra butter and a little more broth at the end of cooking time.

beer-battered fish & best potato wedges

It is such a treat for people with celiac disease to be able to eat fish and chips that taste even better than those bought at the local fish and chip shop. This batter is light and crisp. Prepare the wedges first so that they are ready by the time you have cooked the fish.

SERVES 4

4 large firm white fish filets, each cut into 4 sticks

best potato wedges

1 cup **GF** bread crumbs*

¼ cup grated Parmesan cheese

6 medium Desiree or Sebago potatoes, or 10 large fingerling potatoes, cut into wedges

2 tablespoons melted butter

2 tablespoons oil

beer batter

¼ cup white rice flour

¼ cup pure maize cornstarch

⅓ cup besan (chickpea flour)

1 teaspoon **GF** baking powder

½ teaspoon salt

1 large egg, lightly beaten

½ cup **GF** beer (I use O'Brien Pale Ale)

additional ingredients

bran, canola, or vegetable oil, for shallow-frying fish

pure maize cornstarch, extra, for coating fish

lemon wedges, to serve

line two baking sheets with parchment paper. One baking sheet is for the wedges. Place a wire rack on the second baking sheet.

preheat oven to 400°F.

combine bread crumbs and Parmesan. Season with salt and freshly ground black pepper. Brush potato wedges with combined butter and oil and sprinkle crumb mixture all over. Place on the baking sheet. Bake for 30 minutes until crisp and golden.

reduce the oven temperature to 325°F so it is ready for the batches of fish to be kept warm after frying.

sift flours, baking powder, and salt into a bowl. Make a well in the center and add egg. Whisk gently to incorporate and gradually add beer. Whisk well to combine.

heat oil for frying in a medium–sized skillet.

dust fish with extra cornstarch to coat. This is so the batter sticks to the fish. Dip a piece of fish in the batter and then drag it up the side of the bowl to remove excess batter. Place gently in oil and repeat with remaining fish. Cook a few pieces at a time for 2–3 minutes or until cooked. Place fish on the prepared wire rack and keep warm in the oven until all of the fish is cooked.

serve fish and wedges with lemon and/or **quick tartare sauce** (page 201).

SAVORY SECRETS

GF bread crumbs* see **cook's tips—bread** (page 210).

To make **sumac squid** follow beer batter recipe above and add 1 teaspoon sumac*. Dust squid pieces with pure maize cornstarch then dip in sumac batter and fry. Serve with **cheat's lime mayonnaise** (page 201).

Sumac* is a Lebanese lemon-scented spice with a rich earthy color. It goes well with fish, squid, chicken, and lamb, sprinkled over hummus or in pilaf.

crunchy-crusted snapper with beurre blanc

You can prepare the snapper completely ahead of time so that it's just a matter of popping it in the oven when you are ready to eat. Remember to remove the snapper from the refrigerator 30 minutes before baking. Beurre blanc is a delicious white butter sauce.

SERVES 4

4 skinless snapper filets or other thick-fleshed fish filets

1–2 tablespoons melted butter, to brush fish

olive oil, to drizzle

crunch

1 cup **GF** bread crumbs*

¼ cup blanched almonds or other nuts, chopped

¼ cup unsalted butter, softened

1½ tablespoons chopped herbs—use a mixture of parsley with dill or tarragon

finely grated of zest of 1 lemon, lime, or grapefruit

beurre blanc

¼ cup white wine vinegar

½ cup dry white wine

⅓ cup peeled and very finely chopped French shallots (eschalots)

1 tablespoon whipping cream

⅔ cup cold unsalted butter, cut into small dice

line a baking sheet with parchment paper.

preheat oven to 400°F.

combine crunch ingredients in a bowl. Season with salt and freshly ground black pepper. Blend butter in with your fingers.

place snapper filets on the baking sheet and brush all sides lightly with melted butter. Press crunch on top of the fish and drizzle with a little olive oil.

bake snapper for about 10–12 minutes or until crunch is golden and snapper is cooked. Timing will depend on the thickness of the fish. Prepare sauce while fish is baking.

place vinegar, wine, and shallots in a small saucepan, bring to a boil, and reduce to 2 tablespoons. Strain reduction using a fine sieve, pressing down on the solids to extract as much liquid as possible. Discard solids. Return liquid to saucepan, add cream, and bring to a boil. Remove from the heat and whisk in butter, piece by piece, until sauce thickens. Do not reheat as sauce may split. Season with salt and white pepper. Serve warm with the snapper filets.

serving suggestions
Serve with sautéed English spinach and a few baby vegetables.

SAVORY SECRETS
GF bread crumbs* see **cook's tips—bread** (page 210).

Serve beurre blanc with broiled fish, poultry, beef, lamb, or steamed vegetables.

A squeeze of lemon juice may be added to the beurre blanc, if desired.

polenta, coconut, & lime-coated fish

SERVES 4

4 medium firm white fish filets, cut into even-sized thick fingers (sticks)

polenta, coconut, & lime coating

½ cup fine (one-minute) polenta

½ cup pure maize cornstarch

½ cup shredded coconut

finely grated zest of 2 limes

additional ingredients

½ cup pure maize cornstarch, extra

1 large egg

½ cup whole milk

vegetable or bran oil, for shallow-frying

combine ingredients for the polenta, coconut, & lime coating and set aside.

place extra cornstarch on a plate.

make an egg wash by whisking egg and milk together in a shallow bowl.

roll fish in cornstarch, turning to coat both sides, and shaking off any excess. Dip in egg wash and then press coating ingredients on both sides. Place coated fish on a plate and refrigerate until required. Remove from refrigerator 30 minutes before cooking.

heat about ½ inch oil in a skillet over medium heat. Cook fish in batches. Timing will depend on thickness of the fish. Wipe skillet with kitchen paper after frying each batch of fish. Add more oil as necessary. Keep the fish warm in a preheated oven at 325°F.

serving suggestions
Serve with **hot & spicy corn & avocado salsa** (page 146), baby English spinach leaves, and crème fraîche.

SAVORY SECRET
Substitute chicken underbreast filets for the fish filets.

sesame-glazed salmon with pickled ginger rice

The combination of sesame oil, ginger, and cumin teamed with pickled ginger rice makes this one of my favorite fish recipes. It is cooked at a low temperature in the oven so remains perfectly moist. I love the sweet taste of pickled ginger and it looks so pretty with the contrasting black nigella seeds in the rice.

SERVES 4

4 x 6 ounce salmon filets, skin on

olive oil, for brushing fish before cooking

marinade for the salmon

1 tablespoon ginger syrup, from a jar or vacuum pack of pink pickled ginger*, chopped

1 tablespoon sesame oil

2 teaspoons **GF** tamari

1 tablespoon grated fresh ginger

1 tablespoon light brown sugar

1–2 garlic cloves, crushed

zest of 1 lime, finely grated

2 teaspoons ground cumin

pickled ginger rice

1½ cups long-grain white rice

2 makrut (kaffir lime) leaves

⅓ cup pink pickled ginger*, or to taste, thinly sliced

1 tablespoon nigella seeds**, or use black sesame seeds

line a baking sheet with parchment paper.

preheat oven to 235°F.

combine marinade ingredients and rub over salmon. Marinate in the refrigerator for 1–2 hours. Remove from refrigerator 30 minutes before cooking.

cook rice according to packet instructions, adding lime leaves to the water. They will give the rice a wonderful aromatic flavor. When rice is cooked and drained, stir through pickled ginger and nigella seeds. Set aside.

heat a chargrill pan over medium–high heat. Remove salmon from marinade and reserve marinade. Dab salmon with kitchen paper to remove excess marinade. Brush salmon with olive oil and fry for 1 minute each side. Transfer salmon to baking sheet and drizzle with reserved marinade.

bake salmon for 12 minutes or until cooked to your liking.

serve salmon with marinade from the baking sheet, pickled ginger rice, and **asian greens & cucumber salad** (page 130), omitting the radish.

SAVORY SECRETS

Pink pickled ginger* is available from supermarkets in jars or vacuum packs.

Nigella seeds** are available from health-food and speciality stores. They are jet black in color, have an aromatic, smoky flavor, and are popular in Middle Eastern and Indian cookery.

To mold hot pickled ginger rice, place rice in a ramekin, cup, or dariole mold and press it in gently. Invert the container on a dinner plate. Remove container and repeat for remaining serves.

Rice can be prepared ahead of time and reheated in the microwave to serve.

sumac fish with preserved lemon & caper salsa

The zing of lemon is hard to beat when it comes to fish. Here I have doubled up on the flavor with sumac.

SERVES 4

4 filets snapper, blue-eye, or other white-fleshed fish, skin off (about 7 ounces each)

3 teaspoons olive oil

1 tablespoon sumac*

zest of 1 lemon or lime, finely grated

1 tablespoon unsalted butter

2 teaspoons olive oil, extra

1 quantity **preserved lemon & caper salsa** (page 148)

brush fish filets with olive oil.

mix sumac and lemon zest together and sprinkle over the fish.

heat butter and extra olive oil in a large skillet over medium heat and cook fish for 2–3 minutes on each side or until cooked to your liking. Remove fish to a warm plate. Set aside to rest for a few minutes.

serve fish with preserved lemon & caper salsa.

serving suggestions
Serve with potato purée with cooked lentils folded through.

SAVORY SECRETS
Sumac* is a Lebanese lemon-scented spice with a rich earthy color. It goes well with fish, squid, chicken, and lamb, sprinkled over hummus or in pilaf.
Substitute chicken tenderloins for the fish filets.

chicken in red wine with mushrooms & shallots

My daughter Kate is an excellent cook. This year for my birthday dinner she cooked her version of coq au vin. It was such a hit that it has become another family favorite.

SERVES 6

6 chicken leg quarters (leg and thigh portion)

pure maize cornstarch, for dusting

3 tablespoons unsalted butter

8 medium French shallots (eschalots), covered with boiling water for 5 minutes, drained and peeled, or use 12 scallions, trimmed and chopped

1 medium carrot, diced

1 medium celery rib, diced

9 ounces Swiss brown mushrooms, halved or quartered, depending on size

1⅓ cups chopped **GF** pancetta or **GF** bacon

2 garlic cloves, crushed

¼ cup brandy

1¼ cups good-quality dry red wine

1¼ cups **GF** chicken broth

2 tablespoons **GF** concentrated tomato purée

2 bay leaves

6 sprigs each flat-leaf (Italian) parsley and thyme, tied together in a bundle with cooking twine

2 strips of lemon peel, pith removed

choose a large deep flameproof casserole dish with a tight-fitting lid.

preheat oven to 315°F.

season chicken with freshly ground black pepper and dust lightly all over with cornstarch.

melt butter in the casserole dish over medium heat and brown chicken in batches. Remove chicken to a large bowl. Add shallots, carrot, celery, and mushrooms to dish and cook until shallots are lightly browned. Add pancetta and garlic and cook briefly. Remove to the large bowl with the chicken.

add brandy to dish and cook until it has almost evaporated. Add wine and bring to a boil. Stir and scrape up any brown residue on the base of the dish. Add broth and tomato purée and stir to blend.

add chicken and vegetable mixture, bay leaves, herbs, and lemon peel. Bring to a simmer. Place a piece of parchment paper on top and press down lightly. This prevents evaporation and keeps the casserole from drying out. Cover with casserole dish lid and bake in the oven for 1–1½ hours or until chicken is very tender.

cool see **cook's tips—cooling** (page 211) and refrigerate casserole. When fat sets, remove with spoon and discard. Warm casserole on the stovetop, as the sauce will have jellied. As soon as the jelly melts, remove the chicken and reserve. Boil sauce rapidly to reduce. Return chicken to sauce and reheat to serve.

serving suggestions
Serve with parsnip and potato purée, **crisp parsnip ribbons or "spaghetti"** (page 154), and a green vegetable.

SAVORY SECRETS
This recipe can be cooked a day or two in advance and reheated to serve.
You can make a cornstarch paste to thicken the sauce if you wish.
Add 1 tablespoon drained capers to the recipe towards the end of cooking time.

chicken poached in ginger broth

You can feel this broth doing you good! The broth sits comfortably as a starter or main course.
I prefer to use a well-reduced home-made chicken broth to make it.

4 skinless, boneless chicken breasts, trimmed
of fat and sinew

ginger broth

6 cups well-reduced **GF** chicken broth

3 makrut (kaffir lime) leaves

2-inch piece fresh ginger, peeled and sliced

2 lemon grass stems, bruised

4 star anise

2 garlic cloves, sliced

1 red chile, seeded and sliced on an angle,
to taste

additional ingredients

7 ounces rice stick noodles

1 red chile, extra, seeded and thinly sliced,
to finish

GF soy sauce and/or **GF** fish sauce,
served separately

accompaniments

Crisp-fried shredded ginger, cilantro leaves,
Vietnamese mint, lime wedges, or thinly sliced
red pepper poached in the broth. Wok-fried
or blanched pak choy.

place ingredients for the ginger broth in a large saucepan or small stockpot and bring to a boil. Reduce heat to medium and simmer for 15 minutes. Strain ginger broth through a fine sieve, into a large bowl. Reserve star anise (optional) and discard remaining solids. Return broth to saucepan.

poach chicken breasts very gently in the broth for about 5 minutes or until cooked through.

place rice noodles in a saucepan of boiling water and cook for 3–4 minutes or until softened. Do not overcook noodles as they tend to break up. Cook the noodles while the chicken is poaching.

remove chicken from broth to a chopping board and thinly slice on an angle. To avoid burning your hands wear latex gloves.

drain rice noodles well and divide among heated bowls. Place sliced chicken on top of noodles. Strain the ginger broth again over the chicken and noodles. Finish with extra chile and one star anise per serve, if desired. Choose from any of the accompaniments below.

chicken tagine with lemon & olives

Exotically flavored with spices, preserved lemon, and olives, this easy recipe will bring the sunny taste of Morocco to your table.

SERVES 4

2 tablespoons olive oil

1 large onion, thinly sliced

1 garlic clove, crushed

1½ tablespoons **GF** tagine spice mix*

8 skinless, boneless chicken thighs, trimmed of fat and sinew

1 cup **GF** chicken broth

finely grated zest of 1 orange

⅓ cup orange juice, strained

2 ripe tomatoes, cored and finely chopped

1 tablespoon finely chopped preserved lemon** peel (rinse the preserved lemon first, discard the pulp, and use the peel only)

½ cup stuffed green olives***

cilantro leaves, to finish

toasted almonds or pine nuts, to finish

choose a large skillet with a lid or a risotto pan.

heat 1 tablespoon oil in a large skillet and sauté onion over medium–low heat for 5 minutes. Add garlic and cook briefly. Remove onions and garlic to a bowl and set aside.

combine spice mix and freshly ground black pepper and pat all over chicken. Roll chicken up and secure with toothpicks or cooking twine.

add remaining oil to the skillet and brown chicken rolls. Add onion and garlic mixture, broth, zest, juice, tomato, and preserved lemon. Cover skillet with lid, reduce heat to low, and simmer for 10 minutes. Turn chicken and cook for another 10 minutes or until cooked through.

remove chicken to a large plate and cover loosely with foil to keep warm. Remove toothpicks or twine.

boil sauce uncovered for 5–7 minutes to reduce. Add olives and return chicken to sauce, then simmer to reheat. Finish with cilantro and nuts.

serving suggestions
Serve with **saffron pilaf with vermicelli** (page 205). A side dish of grilled eggplant or **roasted red pepper** (page 164) works well too.

SAVORY SECRETS
Tagine spice mix* is a Moroccan spice blend available in some supermarkets, health-food, and speciality stores.

Chickpeas make a terrific addition to this recipe.

Preserved lemons** are available in supermarkets or prepare **preserved lemons** (page 202).

You could use chicken pieces and allow longer cooking time.

Use almond- or pimento-stuffed green olives***.

duck breasts with saffron ginger glaze

The honey and saffron give the glaze a beautiful golden hue.

SERVES 4

4 boneless duck breasts, skin on

2 teaspoons **GF** Chinese five-spice

saffron ginger glaze

¼ cup runny honey

¼ cup dry sherry

½ cup **GF** chicken broth

1 tablespoon lemon or lime juice

1 small red onion, finely chopped

2-inch piece fresh ginger, peeled and finely chopped

4 star anise

1 garlic clove, sliced

1 red chile, seeded and sliced on an angle, to taste

generous pinch of saffron threads

choose a skillet that is suitable for both stovetop cooking and oven use. Alternatively, line a baking sheet with parchment paper.

preheat oven to 400°F.

score fat on duck in a criss-cross pattern using a thin-bladed knife. Season with salt and freshly ground black pepper. Sprinkle five-spice all over duck filets and set aside.

combine ingredients for the saffron ginger glaze in a small saucepan and simmer for 15 minutes. Remove star anise and reserve. Strain glaze through a fine sieve and press down on the onions to extract as much juice as possible. Discard the solids. Return glaze to saucepan and bring to a boil, then lower heat to achieve a rapid simmer. Reduce glaze to ½ cup. This will take about 10 minutes. Add all four star anise to the glaze and set aside.

heat a skillet over medium heat and cook duck breasts, skin side down, for 3 minutes. Do not add any fat to the pan as scoring the skin helps to render the fat. Turn duck over and cook for 1 minute. Pour off fat from the pan and reserve—see savory secrets below.

transfer duck to the oven or place on a baking sheet. Bake for 6–8 minutes or until done to your liking. Remove from the oven to a warm plate and rest for 5 minutes. If duck skin is not crisp, pop under the broiler, preheated to high, for 1 minute just before serving.

slice duck breasts on an angle. To avoid burning your hands wear latex gloves. Serve with glaze and one star anise per serve.

serving suggestions

Serve with steamed pak choy, yard-long beans, or whole green beans.
Rice cooked by absorption method with 2 makrut (kaffir lime) leaves added to the water or **GF** chicken broth. Place cooked rice in ramekin or dariole mold and turn out on to plates. Top rice with scallions sliced on an angle.

SAVORY SECRETS

The glaze can be prepared several days in advance and refrigerated.

The glaze can be served with chicken, pork, or quail.

The reserved duck fat can be used for roasting potatoes.

gremolata-stuffed chicken

This Italian salsa is traditionally served sprinkled over dishes such as osso buco, but here I've played with the ingredients to create a moist, tangy stuffing for chicken. It is also delicious served cold.

SERVES 4

4 boneless chicken breasts, skin on, or 4 chicken leg quarters (leg and thigh portion), skin on

gremolata stuffing

1 cup flat-leaf (Italian) parsley, roughly chopped

1 tablespoon baby capers, rinsed well if salted and drained on kitchen paper

2 garlic cloves, crushed

1½ tablespoons finely chopped preserved lemon* peel (rinse the preserved lemon first, discard the pulp, and use the peel only)

2 tablespoons unsalted butter, softened

additional ingredients

1 tablespoon unsalted butter, melted

2 teaspoons bran or vegetable oil

line a baking sheet with parchment paper.

preheat oven to 350°F.

place ingredients for the gremolata stuffing in a bowl and rub in butter using your fingers.

separate skin from chicken by pushing your fingers or rolling the handle of a wooden spoon under the skin to lift and separate it from the flesh. Spread a quarter of the stuffing under the skin of each breast or leg quarter. Pat the skin back to its original shape. Brush chicken liberally with additional combined butter and oil. Season with freshly ground black pepper.

heat a skillet over medium–high heat and brown chicken skin-side down, then turn chicken and brown the other side. Transfer chicken to the baking sheet and pour over any remaining butter mixture from the skillet. Bake chicken breasts for about 12 minutes or leg quarters for 30 minutes or until cooked through.

remove chicken from oven and cover loosely with foil. Rest chicken for a few minutes before serving. Slice each breast on an angle in half or in slices. Serve chicken leg quarters whole. Drizzle with pan juices to finish.

serving suggestions
Serve with **cheesy soft polenta** (page 203), roasted vine-ripened tomatoes, and grilled zucchini.

SAVORY SECRETS
Preserved lemons* are available in supermarkets or prepare **preserved lemons** (page 202).

Chicken can be prepared in advance and refrigerated until required. Remove from refrigerator 30 minutes before cooking.

To make **whole chicken with gremolata stuffing** use your fingers or roll the handle of a wooden spoon under the skin to lift and separate it from the flesh. Push stuffing under the skin, down the legs and thighs, and under the breast. Roast chicken in the oven at 400°F for 1–1½ hours depending on the size of the chicken. The stuffing keeps the chicken beautifully moist.

icky sticky chicken legs

This is a very easy recipe that can be prepared several hours before eating. The chicken legs make delicious picnic food. They can be baked in the oven or grilled.

SERVES 4

8–10 large free-range chicken legs

icky sticky marinade

1 garlic clove, crushed

¼ cup bran or vegetable oil

2 teaspoons sesame oil

1 tablespoon grated fresh ginger

finely grated zest and juice of 1 lime or lemon

1 tablespoon runny honey or light brown sugar

1 tablespoon **GF** tamari or **GF** Worcestershire sauce

1 tablespoon **GF** sweet chile sauce

2 tablespoons **GF** tomato ketchup

1 tablespoon Japanese rice vinegar

2 teaspoons ground cumin

additional ingredient

sesame seeds, to sprinkle

line a shallow baking pan with parchment paper.

preheat oven to 350°F.

combine ingredients for the marinade in a glass or ceramic dish or stainless steel bowl. Add the chicken and marinate in the refrigerator for 1½–2 hours or overnight. Alternatively, place chicken and marinade in a large zip-lock plastic bag to marinate. Remove from refrigerator 30 minutes before cooking.

remove chicken legs from marinade and place in the baking pan. Reserve marinade. Sprinkle legs with sesame seeds and bake for 35–45 minutes or until cooked through. Baste with reserved marinade once or twice during cooking. You can add any remaining marinade to the baking pan towards the end of cooking time. Allow marinade to bubble in the dish and serve it over the chicken.

serving suggestions

Serve with rice or rice noodles and **asian greens & cucumber salad** (page 130), if serving chicken hot, or **sweet & spicy mango salsa** (page 148), if serving chicken cold.

SAVORY SECRETS

Substitute chicken wings for the chicken legs. The marinade (omit tomato ketchup) works very well with quail too.

To grill the chicken legs, preheat grill to low–medium heat and brush with oil. Grill chicken legs, turning often so that they do not burn. Baste with marinade. Cooking time will depend on the size of the chicken legs. Boil any remaining marinade in a small saucepan or in the microwave and serve it over the chicken. Add a little water if necessary.

orange marmalade duck ragout

This is a wonderful, rich, and satisfying way to enjoy duck.

SERVES 4–6

4–6 duck leg quarters (leg and thigh portion)

1 large onion, finely diced

1 medium carrot, finely diced

1 medium celery rib, finely diced

6 Swiss brown mushrooms, thickly sliced

2 garlic cloves, crushed

2 cups red wine

2 cups **GF** chicken broth

2 tablespoons **GF** concentrated tomato purée

1 tablespoon orange marmalade

finely grated zest and juice of 1 orange

2 bay leaves

6 juniper berries*, lightly crushed

1 tablespoon thyme leaves

flat-leaf (Italian) parsley, to finish

heat a large flameproof casserole dish over medium heat. Season duck with freshly ground black pepper and cook, in batches if necessary, for 3 minutes. Turn legs over and cook for a further 3 minutes. Remove duck from casserole dish and set aside briefly.

add onion, carrot, celery, and mushrooms to the dish and cook, stirring, for 3 minutes. Add garlic and cook briefly. There will be fat residue from searing the duck so do not add more.

add wine and bring to a boil. Add broth, tomato paste, marmalade, zest, juice, bay leaves, juniper berries, thyme, and duck. Reduce heat to low and simmer partially covered for 1½–2 hours until meat is almost falling off the bone.

remove duck to a plate and cool. Remove meat from the bones. Discard skin and bones. Cover duck meat and place in refrigerator.

cool sauce (see **cook's tips—cooling** (page 210)) and refrigerate. When fat sets, remove and discard it. Boil sauce rapidly over high heat to reduce by half. Skim froth from the surface and discard.

return reserved duck meat to sauce and fold in gently. Reheat to serve.

serving suggestions
Serve over buttered **GF** fettuccine sprinkled with parsley or with **cheesy soft polenta** (page 203) and a side of **green beans with hazelnut oil & roasted hazelnuts** (page 156).

SAVORY SECRETS

Juniper berries* are the fruit of an evergreen tree. When ripe and dried they impart a distinctive sweet-sharp taste. Juniper berries are available in the spice section in most supermarkets.

The ragout can be prepared a day or two in advance and refrigerated or may be frozen.

To vary ragout, add some cooked brown lentils after reducing the sauce.

To make **slow-cooked lamb shanks** substitute 4–6 French-trimmed lamb shanks for the duck leg quarters. Brown shanks in butter and oil and prepare sauce as above. Preheat oven to 300°F and bake shanks in a covered casserole dish for 2–3 hours until tender. Cool shanks and discard fat. Remove shanks and reduce sauce by boiling rapidly over high heat. Return shanks to sauce and reheat. Serve with potato or parsnip purée and a green vegetable.

prosciutto–wrapped chicken with leek & ricotta

I love anything that can be prepared in advance and then baked with a minimum of fuss.

SERVES 4

1 tablespoon unsalted butter

2 teaspoons olive oil, plus extra, for brushing

4 boneless, skinless chicken breasts, underbreast filet removed to use in another recipe or freeze

2 small leeks, white part only, trimmed, rinsed well, and thinly sliced

1 garlic clove, crushed

⅓ cup ricotta cheese, drained in a kitchen-paper-lined colander

⅓ cup grated Parmesan cheese

2 tablespoons chopped flat-leaf (Italian) parsley

8 thin prosciutto slices (4 slices may be enough depending on how long and wide they are)

line a baking sheet with parchment paper.

preheat oven to 350°F.

heat butter and oil in a large skillet over high heat. Season chicken with freshly ground black pepper and brown quickly on both sides. Remove from pan to a plate.

sauté leeks in the same skillet over medium heat until softened. Add garlic and cook briefly. Cool a little.

combine ricotta, Parmesan, and parsley with cooled leeks.

cut a pocket about 2 inches deep along the side of each chicken breast with a sharp knife. Fill each pocket with a quarter of the ricotta filling. Roll meat back over the filling to close the pocket.

wrap each chicken breast in prosciutto, brush with extra olive oil, and place on the baking sheet.

bake for 12–15 minutes or until cooked through. Allow chicken to rest for a few minutes before serving whole or slice each breast in half on an angle.

serving suggestions
Serve with pan juices or **easy tomato sauce** (page 200), sautéed mushrooms, and baby English spinach leaves.

SAVORY SECRET
Chicken may be prepared up to 8 hours in advance and refrigerated. Remove from refrigerator 30 minutes before baking.

sage & citrus quail

Ask your butcher to bone or butterfly the quail if you are not up to it. Place finger bowls on the table if quail is not boned. You can also prepare **last-minute chicken** using the marinade (see "Savory secrets").

SERVES 4

6 quail, boned or butterflied (see note)

marinade

¼ cup) olive oil, plus extra, for brushing

1 tablespoon brandy

2 teaspoons runny honey

1 garlic clove, crushed

finely grated zest and juice of 1 small orange

finely grated zest of 1 lime or lemon

1 tablespoon lime or lemon juice

3 teaspoons finely chopped sage leaves, or use rosemary or thyme

combine ingredients for the marinade in a glass or stainless steel bowl. Reserve 2 tablespoons of marinade to drizzle over quail after cooking.

marinate quail and place in the refrigerator for 1–1½ hours. Turn once during this time.

preheat an outdoor grill to medium. Brush grill with oil. Grill quail skin-side down for 3–4 minutes. Brush with marinade then turn and cook other side for 3 minutes or until cooked through. Boned quail don't take long to cook at all. Allow 4–5 minutes each side if quail is not boned.

remove quail to a warm plate, drizzle with reserved marinade, cover loosely with foil, and rest for 5–10 minutes before serving.

note: Use poultry shears or kitchen scissors to cut either side of the backbone. Discard backbone. Open quail out and press down to crack bones so they lie flat. Rinse and pat dry with kitchen paper. Cut the quail in half if you wish.

serving suggestions
Serve with marinade and **blood orange, fennel, & olive salad** (page 138) or **lemon & parsley potatoes** (page 161).

SAVORY SECRET
To make **last-minute chicken** you will need 4 boneless, skinless chicken breasts. Slice each chicken breast into three thin escalopes or place them one at a time in a large freezer bag then pound thick end lightly with a meat mallet or rolling pin to flatten to ½ inch thickness. Cut each pounded chicken breast into three even-sized pieces. Prepare the marinade above, reserving several tablespoons to drizzle over the chicken after cooking. Marinate chicken for about ½–1 hour. Preheat grill to medium. Brush grill with oil and cook chicken for about 3 minutes on each side or until cooked through.

spatchcock with cranberry & pistachio stuffing

I prepared this stuffing for my Christmas turkey and loved it so much I now use it to stuff spatchcock (poussin) too. The spatchcock are quite large when stuffed. You can serve half per person if you wish. Use an electric knife to cut the spatchcock in half.

SERVES 4–8

4 x 1 pound 2 ounce spatchcock (poussin), cavity rinsed and wiped with kitchen paper

cranberry & pistachio stuffing

1 tablespoon olive oil

1 small onion, finely diced

1 medium celery rib, finely diced

1 **GF** bacon slice, chopped

1 garlic clove, crushed

1½ tablespoons unsalted butter

1½ cups **GF** bread crumbs*

zest of 1 orange, finely grated

1½ tablespoons finely chopped preserved lemon** peel (rinse the preserved lemon first, discard the pulp, and use the peel only)

¼ cup flat-leaf (Italian) parsley, chopped

1 tablespoon fresh thyme leaves

⅔ cup sweetened dried cranberries

¼ cup unsalted pistachio nuts

1 large egg, lightly beaten

additional ingredients

extra olive oil and melted butter, combined

1–2 onions, cut into ¼ inch slices

pan sauce

½ teaspoon **GF** mustard powder

¼ cup white wine

½ cup **GF** chicken broth

a splash of whipping cream

grease the base of a large flameproof baking dish.

preheat oven to 400 F.

heat oil in a skillet over medium heat and sauté onion and celery until softened. Add bacon and garlic and cook briefly. Add butter to the pan to melt. Set aside.

combine bread crumbs, zest, lemon, herbs, carnberries, and pistachios in a large bowl and stir in onion and bacon mixture. Add egg to bind and season with freshly ground black pepper. Cool stuffing before spooning into spatchcock cavities. Tie legs together with cooking twine. Brush spatchcock with extra olive oil and butter mixture and season with freshly ground black pepper.

place sliced onions in the baking dish and rest spatchcock on top. Bake for 45 minutes or until cooked through. Test with a skewer by inserting it in the thickest part of the thigh. The juices should run clear. Transfer the spatchcock to a large warm plate, cover with foil, and leave to rest.

spoon excess fat from baking dish. Place over medium heat. Stir in mustard, deglaze dish with wine, and bring to a boil. Stir and scrape up any brown residue on the base. Add broth and cook for several minutes. Strain contents through a fine sieve over a bowl, pressing down on the onions to extract as much flavor as possible. Discard onions. Return sauce to dish or a small saucepan. Warm sauce and add cream to finish. Transfer sauce to a pitcher to serve.

serving suggestions
Serve with **roughed-up roasted potatoes** (page 166) and snow peas or asparagus. Pan sauce and/or cranberry sauce.

SAVORY SECRETS
GF bread crumbs* see **cook's tips—bread** (page 210).

Preserved lemons** are available in supermarkets or prepare **preserved lemons** (page 202).

Make extra stuffing, bake in a bar tin, and enjoy with leftover turkey or chicken in a salad or sandwich with cranberry sauce and/or **GF** mayonnaise.

spicy chicken

This quick and versatile recipe can be served with a summer salad. It also makes a wonderful meal at cooler times of the year.

SERVES 4

1 tablespoon sesame oil

1 tablespoon bran or grape seed oil

1 garlic clove, crushed

1 pound chicken underbreast filets, trimmed of fat or sinew

1 teaspoon fennel seeds, crushed to a fine powder using a mortar and pestle

1 teaspoon cumin seeds, crushed to a fine powder using a mortar and pestle

1 teaspoon **GF** Chinese five-spice

1 teaspoon ground ginger

¼ teaspoon ground chile powder or flakes, to taste

½ teaspoon sugar

additional ingredients

2 tablespoons unsalted butter

1 tablespoon bran or grape seed oil

combine sesame oil, bran oil, and garlic in a bowl. Add chicken and stir thoroughly to coat.

place chicken on a large plate in a single layer.

combine fennel, cumin, Chinese five-spice, ginger, chile, sugar, and salt and pepper to taste in a small bowl. Pat spice mixture on both sides of the chicken.

heat a skillet over medium heat and add half the butter and oil. Cook chicken in two batches. The underbreast filets will take about 2 minutes on each side to cook. Remove to a warm plate. Wipe pan with kitchen paper. Add remaining butter and oil and cook second batch of chicken.

serving suggestions

Serve with **baby spinach & mango salad with lime drizzle** (page 134). The meal can be plated individually or served on one large platter if you are catering for a crowd. Alternatively, prepare **saffron pilaf with vermicelli** (page 205). When pilaf is cooked, stir in some sliced dried apricots, pistachio nuts, and chopped cilantro leaves to finish. You can serve a side bowl of **GF** Greek-style yogurt combined with 1 teaspoon sumac too, if you wish.

beef & mushroom hotpot

This rich hotpot meal is the ultimate comfort food on a cold winter's night. I just love the aroma that comes from the oven while it is cooking, slow and steady. It really gets my taste buds excited.

SERVES 4–6

1 tablespoon olive oil

2 tablespoons unsalted butter (you may need a little more)

2 medium onions, cut into quarters

7 ounces Swiss brown mushrooms, halved or quartered, depending on size

2 garlic cloves, crushed

3 pounds 5 ounces beef bolar (see note), chuck, or rump, in one piece, tied with cooking twine

2 cups full-bodied red wine

2 tablespoons **GF** Dijon mustard

1½ tablespoons redcurrant jelly

1 tablespoon **GF** Worcestershire sauce

1 **GF** chicken bouillon cube, crumbled

6 thyme sprigs

2 bay leaves

¼ cup roughly chopped flat-leaf (Italian) parsley

1 tablespoon pure maize cornstarch, mixed with 2 tablespoons water, to thicken

choose a large deep flameproof casserole dish with a tight-fitting lid.

preheat oven to 300°F.

heat oil and butter in casserole dish over medium–low heat and sauté onions for 5 minutes. Add mushrooms and brown lightly. Add garlic and cook briefly. Remove vegetables to a large bowl and set aside.

season beef with freshly ground black pepper, place in the casserole, and brown well on all sides over high heat. Remove and add to vegetables.

add red wine to the dish and bring to a boil. Add mustard, redcurrant jelly, Worcestershire sauce, bouillon cube, thyme, bay leaves, vegetables, and beef. Cover with lid. Place dish in the oven and bake for 2–3 hours until the beef is very tender—it should be just about falling apart. Turn beef after 1 hour and add half the parsley. When beef is cooked, remove it to a plate using a slotted spoon and cover loosely with foil. Strain sauce over a bowl, reserve vegetables, and discard thyme and bay leaves. Rinse casserole dish.

cool sauce (see **cook's tips—cooling** (page 211)) and refrigerate. When fat sets, remove and discard it. Return sauce to casserole dish. Place over high heat and bring to a rapid boil to reduce the sauce a little. Thicken sauce with the cornstarch paste.

remove twine from beef. Cut off and discard any fat. Pull beef apart into chunks rather than slicing. Return beef and vegetables to dish and simmer gently to reheat.

serve hotpot sprinkled with remaining parsley.

note: Beef bolar is a large cut of meat which comes from the pointed end of the chuck blade. It is more tender than most other blade.

serving suggestions
Serve with boiled new potatoes tossed in melted butter and sprinkled with chives or celeriac purée and a green vegetable.

SAVORY SECRETS
The hotpot may be cooked 2 days in advance.
Substitute quince paste, cut into small pieces, or honey, for the redcurrant jelly.
Substitute **GF** tamari for the **GF** worcestershire sauce.

chile beef with guacamole salsa

Cocoa, chile, and red wine give this dish a delicious rich flavor. I always make this quantity so that I have leftovers for the freezer.

SERVES 8–10

1 quantity **guacamole salsa** (page 146)

chile beef

1 tablespoon bran oil

2 medium onions, thinly sliced

1 medium red pepper, deseeded, membrane removed, flesh diced

2 garlic cloves, crushed

1 hot chile, finely chopped, to taste

2 pounds 4 ounces lean ground beef

½ cup red wine

1 cup **GF** chicken or **GF** beef broth

2 bay leaves

2 x 14 ounce cans chopped tomatoes

4 tablespoons **GF** concentrated tomato purée

2 teaspoons light brown sugar

2 tablespoons unsweetened cocoa powder (I use Dutch cocoa)

2 tablespoons harissa paste*, or to taste

2 teaspoons mixed dried herbs

14 ounce can red kidney beans, drained and rinsed

4½ ounce can chickpeas, drained and rinsed

prepare guacamole salsa and set aside.

heat a large skillet over medium heat. Add oil and sauté onions and pepper until softened. Add garlic and chile and cook briefly. Remove to a large bowl.

increase heat to high and brown beef in batches. Do not add too much beef at a time as it will stew rather than brown. Add browned beef to the onion and pepper.

deglaze pan with wine and bring to a boil. Add broth, bay leaves, tomatoes, tomato paste, sugar, cocoa, harissa paste, herbs, and the beef, onion, and pepper mixture. Bring to a boil then reduce heat to low and simmer for 40 minutes or until well reduced.

add red kidney beans and chickpeas and heat through to serve.

serving suggestions
Serve with guacamole salsa, sour cream, and **chickpea flat bread** (page 14).

SAVORY SECRETS
Harissa paste* is a traditional accompaniment to Tunisian dishes. It is a vibrant red, hot paste made with chile. It is available in supermarkets and speciality stores.

If your children do not like whole beans, you can purée half the beans and stir in with the remainder so even if they pick out the whole beans they will still get some nutrients from the "hidden" puréed beans!

crepe lasagne

Lasagne made with crepes makes a very nice change from the traditional lasagne pasta sheets. It is not as heavy on the tummy either. I've replaced béchamel sauce with layers of quick cheesy ricotta.

SERVES 6

1 quantity **herbed crepes** (page 207)

quick cheesy ricotta

3 cups ricotta cheese, drained in a kitchen-paper-lined colander

3 large eggs, lightly beaten

1 cup grated Parmesan cheese

bolognese sauce

1 tablespoon olive oil

1 medium onion, finely diced

1 medium carrot, grated

1 medium celery rib, finely diced

1 red or green pepper, deseeded, membrane removed, flesh finely diced

2 **GF** bacon slices, finely diced

1 or 2 garlic cloves, crushed

1 bay leaf

1 pound 2 ounces lean ground beef

¾ cup red or white wine

14 ounce can chopped tomatoes

2 tablespoons **GF** concentrated tomato purée

1 **GF** bouillon cube, crumbled

1 teaspoon sugar

1 teaspoon dried oregano

2 tablespoons chopped flat-leaf (Italian) parsley

additional ingredients

grated Parmesan cheese, extra

freshly grated nutmeg, to finish

grease a 10 inch spring-form cake pan and line the base and side with parchment paper.

preheat oven to 350°F.

prepare herbed crepes.

combine ricotta, eggs, and Parmesan in a bowl. Set aside.

heat oil in a skillet over medium–low heat. Add onion, carrot, celery, and pepper and cook gently for 3 minutes. Add bacon, garlic, and bay leaf and cook briefly. Transfer to a large bowl. Increase heat to high and add beef in batches, crumbling it into the pan. Use a fork to break it up. Do not overcrowd pan or the beef will stew instead of browning. When beef has browned, add to vegetable and bacon mixture. Repeat until you have browned all the beef.

add wine to the pan and bring to a boil. Stir and scrape any brown residue on the base of the pan. Add tomato, 1 cup water, tomato paste, bouillon cube, sugar, herbs, and beef mixture. Season with freshly ground black pepper. Simmer sauce for 35–40 minutes until well reduced. It is important for the sauce to be very firm to layer well in the crepes. Cool sauce.

remove the side of the spring-form pan and set aside. Place one crepe on the lined bottom of the cake pan and spread with a quarter of the bolognese sauce. Top with a second crepe. Spread this crepe with a quarter of the quick cheesy ricotta and top with a third crepe. Continue to layer the lasagne until you have used all of the bolognese sauce, cheesy ricotta, and crepes. Finish with a layer of cheesy ricotta and sprinkle with extra Parmesan and nutmeg. Place the lined spring-form side around the crepe lasagne and secure. Place the crepe lasagne on a baking sheet.

bake for about 1 hour until golden on top. Rest for 10 minutes before removing spring-form side. Cut into wedges, using a thin-bladed knife, to serve.

serving suggestions

Serve with a green salad, shaved Parmesan, and olives. Dress salad with olive oil and balsamic vinegar.

SAVORY SECRETS

The herbed crepes and bolognese sauce can be made in advance and frozen.

The bolognese sauce can also be served over **GF** spaghetti.

greek beef or lamb kabobs

I spent two months travelling around the Greek Islands and ate my fair share of souvlaki. I still love kabobs as they are easy to prepare ahead of time and quick to barbecue.

SERVES 4

1 pound beef rump or boneless lamb loin, trimmed of fat and sinew and cut into 1 inch cubes

marinade

2 tablespoons olive oil, plus a little extra, to drizzle over kabobs before cooking

¼ cup red wine

finely grated zest of 1 lemon

1 tablespoon lemon juice

1 small onion, very finely chopped

1–2 garlic cloves, crushed

1 tablespoon dried oregano, or use 1½ tablespoons finely chopped oregano or rosemary

2 bay leaves

vegetables

1 medium red onion, cut into six wedges and separated

1 medium red pepper, deseeded, membrane removed, flesh cut into 1-inch pieces

1 medium green pepper, deseeded, membrane removed, flesh cut into 1-inch pieces

16 button mushrooms, halved if large

soak eight bamboo skewers in water for 30 minutes (to prevent them from burning during cooking) or use metal skewers. Alternatively, use firm rosemary stems stripped of all but a few leaves at the top.

combine the marinade ingredients in a glass or ceramic dish or stainless steel bowl. Marinate meat for 1–2 hours.

preheat an outdoor grill to medium–high.

thread marinated meat, alternating with onion, peppers, and mushrooms, onto the skewers.

drizzle extra oil over kabobs and grill for 2–3 minutes on each side or until done to your liking.

serving suggestions

Serve with steamed rice and a bowl of **GF** Greek-style yogurt combined with crushed garlic and chopped mint.

SAVORY SECRETS

To make **chicken kabobs** substitute white wine for the red wine in the marinade.

Omit the vegetables other than onion from the kabobs and make a **greek salad with a twist** to serve. Combine cherry tomatoes, baby English spinach, sliced marinated artichoke hearts (from a jar), crumbled feta cheese, and black olives. Drizzle salad with olive oil and lemon juice.

herby lamb with blue-green lentils

SERVES 4

¼ cup olive oil

1–2 garlic cloves, crushed

12–16 French-trimmed lamb cutlets or
1 pound 7 ounces boneless lamb loin,
trimmed of fat and sinew

herby lamb rub

finely grated zest of 2 lemons

1½ tablespoons chopped mixed herbs, such
as parsley, rosemary, thyme, and oregano

1 teaspoon mixed dried herbs

1½ teaspoons ground cumin

lentils du puy

1 cup tiny blue-green lentils*, rinsed and
checked for small stones

1 tablespoon unsalted butter

½ medium onion, finely chopped

1 medium celery rib, finely chopped

1 small carrot, finely chopped

1 garlic clove, crushed

1 bay leaf

2 cups **GF** chicken or **GF** vegetable broth

2 tablespoons chopped flat-leaf
(Italian) parsley

additional ingredient

4 ounces soft goat curd, to serve

combine oil and garlic in a small bowl and brush over lamb.

combine ingredients for the herby lamb rub. Pat over lamb and marinate for
1–3 hours or more.

place lentils in a large saucepan, cover with water, and place over medium heat.
Bring to a simmer then drain immediately and reserve lentils. Rinse saucepan.

heat butter in the same saucepan over medium heat. Add onion, celery,
and carrot and sauté until softened. Add garlic and bay leaf and cook briefly,
then add broth and reserved lentils. Bring to a boil and reduce heat to low.
Cover with lid and simmer for 35 minutes or until lentils are tender. If broth has
not been absorbed in this time, remove lid and continue to cook until broth is
absorbed. Add parsley. Season with salt and freshly ground black pepper. Cover
and set aside.

heat a ridged skillet or outdoor grill to medium–high. Cook lamb cutlets for
2–3 minutes each side or lamb loin for 3–4 minutes each side or until cooked
to your liking. Rest lamb, covered loosely with foil, for 5 minutes. Slice lamb loin
across the grain to serve.

serve lamb with lentils and a dollop of goat curd. Serve goat curd separately if
you wish.

serving suggestions
Serve with roasted carrots and/or chargrilled wedges of eggplant or zucchini. Drizzle a
little **demi-glaze** (page 198) or vin cotto** on the plate.

SAVORY SECRETS
The rub can be used with chicken, beef, and lamb.

Tiny blue-green lentils*, also known as lentils du puy, are from Le Puy-en-Velay in the
Auvergne region of France. They are available in health food and speciality stores. Other
fine green lentils may be substituted. You can prepare the lentils in advance and reheat
them in the microwave for 3 minutes on medium heat.

Cook extra lentils to use in **red pepper & lentil potpies with feta crumble** (page 124).

Vin cotto** is an Italian wine vinegar that is available in speciality stores.

italian meatloaf roll with tomato & pepper sauce

This meatloaf roll looks impressive. It is excellent served cold too.

SERVES 6

tomato & pepper sauce

2–3 ripe tomatoes, about 10 ounces in total, or use tin chopped tomatoes

2 teaspoons olive oil

½ cup roasted red pepper (page 164), roughly chopped

½ cup **GF** chicken broth

¼ teaspoon balsamic vinegar

meatloaf roll

½ bunch (9 ounces) English spinach, trimmed and rinsed

2 teaspoons olive oil

1 medium onion, finely chopped

1 garlic clove, crushed

1 pound 10 ounces lean ground beef

4 ounces **GF** spicy salami, ground in a food processor or **GF** bacon, finely chopped

2 cups **GF** bread crumbs*

2 teaspoons dried mixed herbs

2 tablespoons chopped herbs, such as parsley, rosemary and/or oregano

1 large egg

6–8 prosciutto slices, depending on the width of the slices

½ cup semi-dried tomatoes

½ cup pitted Kalamata olives

1 tablespoon capers, rinsed well if salted and drained on kitchen paper

line a baking sheet with parchment paper.

score a cross in the base of each tomato using a sharp knife and blanch in boiling water for 30–60 seconds, peel, then roughly chop. Heat oil in a skillet and sauté tomato until soft. Add remaining ingredients and simmer for 5 minutes. Purée sauce in a food processor. Set aside.

blanch spinach in boiling water and refresh in cold water. Squeeze water from spinach and spread on a clean dish towel. Roll spinach in dish towel to remove excess water. You should be left with 5–6 ounces blanched spinach leaves. Set aside.

heat oil in a small skillet over medium heat and sauté onion until softened. Add garlic and cook briefly, then remove from the heat and cool.

combine onion and garlic with beef, salami, bread crumbs, herbs, and egg in a large bowl. Mix well.

tear a piece of freezer wrap or foil measuring approximately 18 x 13 inches. Place prosciutto slices vertically, slightly overlapping along the freezer wrap or foil. Place meat mixture on top and shape by patting it down into a rectangle measuring approximately 13 x 10 inches.

spread spinach leaves down the center of the mixture leaving a 2 inch border along each long edge. Place semi-dried tomatoes, olives, and capers in rows down the center of the spinach.

preheat oven to 350°F.

roll the mixture into a long meatloaf roll using the freezer wrap or foil as a guide and twist ends. Place meatloaf roll in the refrigerator to firm for 30 minutes. Remove from refrigerator 30 minutes before baking. You can prepare meatloaf up to this stage several hours ahead of cooking.

remove freezer wrap or foil from meatloaf roll and carefully place seam-side down on prepared baking sheet. Bake for 40–45 minutes or until cooked through.

serve meatloaf roll in thick slices with warm tomato & pepper sauce and baked fennel or eggplant.

slow-cooked lamb with raisins & pine nuts

SERVES 6

3 pounds ounces boned lamb leg, cut into 2 inch cubes

finely grated zest of 3 oranges

1¼ cups fresh orange juice, strained

1 tablespoon chopped thyme or rosemary

2 bay leaves

2 garlic cloves, crushed

2 tablespoons deseeded tamarind pulp concentrate*

2 tablespoons unsalted butter

1½ tablespoons olive oil

1 large onion, diced

3 teaspoons za'atar**

2 teaspoons ground cumin

2 teaspoons ground coriander

chile powder or flakes, to taste (optional)

½ cup red wine

1 tablespoon dry sherry

1 **GF** chicken bouillon cube, crumbled

3 tomatoes, diced, or use a 7-ounce can chopped tomatoes

1 tablespoon finely chopped preserved lemon peel (rinse the preserved lemon first and discard the pulp)

½ cup seedless raisins

1 tablespoon pure maize cornstarch mixed with 2 tablespoons water (optional)

¼ cup pine nuts, toasted, to finish

preheat oven to 300°F.

combine lamb, zest, juice, thyme, bay leaves, and garlic in a glass bowl. Marinate for at least 2 hours or preferably overnight. Drain lamb in a colander set over a bowl and reserve marinade. Pat lamb dry with kitchen paper.

soak tamarind in ½ cup hot water. Use your fingers or a fork to break up the pulp. Strain, reserve the purée, and discard fibres. Set aside.

heat 1 teaspoon each of butter and oil in a large skillet over medium heat, sauté onion until softened, add spices, and cook briefly. Remove mixture to a large casserole dish. Add another teaspoon each of butter and oil to the skillet. Season lamb with freshly ground black pepper and brown in batches. Do not overcrowd the pan or the meat will stew. Add lamb to casserole dish after browning each batch.

add wine, sherry, and tamarind to skillet and bring to a boil. Stir and scrape any brown residue from the base of the skillet. Add reserved marinade, crumbled bouillon cube, tomato, and preserved lemon. Pour mixture over lamb. Gently press lamb into the liquid—it should just cover the lamb. If not, add a little water. Place a piece of parchment paper on top and press down lightly to keep the casserole from drying out. Cover dish with lid, place in oven, and cook for 1½ hours. Add raisins and continue to cook for a further 30–60 minutes until lamb is very tender.

cool see **cook's tips—cooling** (page 211) and refrigerate casserole. When fat sets, remove and discard it. Remove lamb from liquid and reserve. Place casserole dish over high heat, bring to a rapid boil, and reduce liquid to about 2 cups. Stir in cornstarchpaste to thicken, if desired. Return lamb to sauce and simmer to reheat. Serve with toasted pine nuts.

serving suggestions
Serve with quinoa or rice and/or **baked winter squash with sweet smoked paprika** (page 150).

SAVORY SECRETS
Tamarind pulp concentrate* or wet tamarind is available in blocks with or without seeds. It comes from a tropical tree native to Africa and is used to flavor sauces, impart acidity to dishes, and also as a thickening agent. It is available from Middle Eastern or Asian grocery stores.

Za'atar** is a traditional Middle Eastern spice blend of thyme, sesame seeds, and sumac. It is available from supermarkets and Middle Eastern or Asian grocery stores.

Preserved lemons*** are available in supermarkets or prepare **preserved lemons** (page 202).

basil pesto pasta with "no-mess" poached eggs

This recipe is quick, easy, and very satisfying. You can make the poached eggs in the traditional way or try my "no-mess" method. The added bonus is that you have only to wipe the saucepan dry!

SERVES 4

basil pesto

2 cups firmly packed basil leaves

2 garlic cloves, crushed

2 tablespoons pine nuts

⅓ cup olive oil

¼ cup grated Parmesan cheese

¼ cup grated Romano cheese

additional ingredients

12 ounces **GF** spaghetti or other **GF** pasta

shaved Parmesan cheese, to serve

baby basil leaves, to serve

"no-mess" poached eggs

4 large eggs, at room temperature

olive oil, to brush

blanch basil quickly in boiling water. Refresh immediately in cold water. Place on kitchen paper or a clean dish towel and gently dab to remove excess water. Blanching basil stops the pesto from discoloring.

place basil, garlic, and pine nuts in a food processor. With motor running, slowly add oil through the feed tube. Add cheeses and continue to process until ingredients are blended.

cook pasta in boiling salted water until *al dente*. While pasta is cooking, prepare poached eggs.

place a large saucepan three-quarters full of water over medium–high heat and bring up to a simmer.

tear a piece of microwave-safe plastic wrap approximately 14 inches long and place it on a work surface. Brush a little olive oil in the center of the plastic and then place it loosely over a small dish. Break one egg into it, gather up the corners of the plastic, remove from dish, and twist plastic into a rope. Loop it through to tie a knot close to the egg. Alternatively, twist the rope and use cooking twine to tie a knot close to the egg. Repeat with remaining eggs.

place eggs in simmering water and cook for about 4 minutes. Lift the eggs with a slotted spoon to feel if they are cooked to your liking. Remove eggs from water and rest on kitchen paper. Leave eggs to sit briefly while you strain the pasta.

strain pasta, reserving 1–2 tablespoons of cooking liquid to add to the pesto. Fold pesto through pasta and divide among heated bowls. To serve the eggs, cut just under the knot with scissors and peel away the plastic. Use a spoon to lift poached eggs and place one on top of each serve of pasta. You can pierce the egg with a knife and let the yolk ooze over the pasta, if you wish. Serve with shaved Parmesan and a baby basil leaves.

SAVORY SECRETS

To vary the pesto, use equal quantities of basil, rocket, and parsley.

If serving "no-mess" poached eggs on toast for breakfast, add a drizzle of truffle oil once you have broken the egg into the plastic wrap. Twist the plastic, tie the "rope", and poach as above.

herbed crepes with spinach & ricotta

These crepes are lovely to serve for brunch or lunch.

MAKES 8 CREPES

1 quantity **herbed crepes** (page 207)

spinach and ricotta filling

1 bunch (1 pound 2 ounces) English spinach, trimmed and rinsed well

1 teaspoon olive oil

1 tablespoon unsalted butter

1 small onion, finely chopped, or use 4 scallions, thinly sliced

1 garlic clove, crushed

2 cups ricotta cheese, drained in a kitchen-paper-lined colander, reserving ¼ cup to spread on top of filled crepes

½ teaspoon freshly grated nutmeg

additional ingredients

grated Parmesan cheese and Cheddar cheese, to finish

freshly grated nutmeg, extra, to finish

pine nuts, toasted, to serve (optional)

line a baking sheet with parchment paper.

preheat oven to 350°F.

prepare herbed crepes. If you have made and frozen the crepes in advance, thaw and then microwave each one for 10 seconds on high heat to soften before filling, otherwise they may crack.

blanch spinach in boiling water and then refresh in cold water. Lightly squeeze water from spinach and spread it on a clean dish towel. Roll spinach in dish towel to remove excess water. You should be left with approximately 10–11 ounces blanched spinach. Chop spinach roughly and set aside.

heat oil and butter in a skillet over medium heat and sauté the onion for about 5 minutes or until soft. Add garlic and cook briefly.

combine ricotta, spinach, onion and garlic mixture, and nutmeg.

place crepes on a work surface. Divide spinach and ricotta mixture among crepes and place it in the center. Make a 3 x 3 inch square with the mixture. Fold crepe over to enclose. Place crepe parcel seam-side down on baking sheet. Spread reserved ricotta on top and sprinkle with combined Parmesan, Cheddar cheese, and nutmeg.

bake for about 15 minutes until cheese is bubbling and golden.

serve crepes with toasted pine nuts scattered over, if desired.

serving suggestions

Serve with **easy tomato sauce** (page 200) with fresh basil, or a side of salad greens, mushrooms, and olives drizzled with olive oil and balsamic vinegar.

SAVORY SECRETS

Herbed crepes with spinach & ricotta can be prepared in advance and frozen or prepared a day in advance, covered with plastic wrap, and refrigerated. Thaw if frozen and remove from refrigerator 30 minutes before baking.

mediterranean vegetable & ricotta gratin

Although this gratin is a vegetarian meal it can also be served with grilled chicken, beef, or lamb.

SERVES 4–6

⅓ cup olive oil

1 garlic clove, crushed

1 large eggplant, cut into ¼ inch slices

14 ounces butternut squash, deseeded, peeled, and cut into ¼ inch slices

4 medium zucchini, cut into long thin strips

2 medium red peppers

2 cups ricotta cheese, drained in a kitchen-paper-lined colander

1 cup grated Parmesan cheese

2 large eggs

1 cup roughly chopped flat-leaf (Italian) parsley

additional ingredients

½ cup grated Parmesan cheese, extra

1 cup **GF** bread crumbs*

olive oil, extra, to drizzle

line 2 or 3 baking sheets with parchment paper.

grease a 9 x 9 x 2 inch square ovenproof dish or similar size rectangular dish and line the base with parchment paper.

preheat oven to 350°F.

combine oil with garlic and brush both sides of vegetable slices lightly with the oil.

place prepared eggplant, squash, and zucchini on baking sheets and bake for 15–20 minutes or until tender. Roast capsicum until skin blisters and blackens. Cool capsicum, peel, remove seeds and membranes, and open out flat.

combine ricotta, Parmesan, eggs, and parsley in a large bowl and season with freshly ground black pepper.

place a layer of eggplant in the base of the ovenproof dish and spread with a thin layer of ricotta mixture. Repeat layering with remaining vegetables, spreading the ricotta mixture between layers and finishing with ricotta mixture on top.

combine extra Parmesan with bread crumbs and sprinkle on top. Drizzle over extra oil.

bake gratin for 35–40 minutes. Place under a preheated broiler to brown for a few minutes if necessary. Rest gratin for 20 minutes before serving.

serving suggestions
Serve with a side of salad greens with black olives and drizzle with olive oil and balsamic vinegar.

SAVORY SECRETS
GF bread crumbs* see **cook's tips—bread** (page 210).

Vegetables can be baked or cooked on an outdoor. They can be prepared 2 days in advance.

You can substitute pecorino or Romano cheese for the Parmesan.

This gratin will keep well for 2 days.

millet pilaf with saffron & green vegetables

Millet is a highly nutritious cereal grain with a delicious nutty taste. It is, of course, gluten-free and easy to digest.

SERVES 4

millet pilaf

2 tablespoons unsalted butter

1 tablespoon olive oil (you may require a little more)

1 onion or leek, white part only, rinsed well, finely chopped

1 celery rib, finely chopped

2 garlic cloves, crushed

2–3 makrut (kaffir lime) leaves

finely grated zest of 1 large lemon

2½ tablespoons lemon juice

1½ cups hulled millet

½ cup dry white wine

4 cups hot **GF** vegetable or **GF** chicken broth (for non-vegetarians)

¼ teaspoon saffron threads

¼ cup currants

additional ingredients

1 bunch asparagus, trimmed and cut into 2½ inch lengths

1 bunch broccolini, cut into 2 inch lengths

1¼ cup snow peas or sugar snap peas

½ cup blanched almonds, toasted

heat butter and oil in a large skillet (with a fitted lid) or use a risotto pan over medium–high heat. Add onion and celery and sauté until softened. Add garlic, makrut leaves, and zest and cook briefly.

add millet and stir until it is well coated with butter and oil mixture. Cook for 2 minutes, moving the millet around the skillet. Add wine and bring to a boil. It will evaporate quickly.

add broth and saffron threads. Season with salt and freshly ground black pepper. Bring to a boil then reduce the heat immediately to low. Cover with lid and simmer gently, undisturbed, for 15 minutes. The millet will absorb all of the broth. At the end of cooking time, add lemon juice and currants. Stir the pilaf gently with a fork. Cover again and leave to rest for 10 minutes.

prepare vegetables and steam or blanch while pilaf is resting.

serve pilaf with steamed vegetables and almonds.

SAVORY SECRETS

Millet pilaf is a good substitute for couscous.

To vary the recipe, prepare millet pilaf as above, adding 1 teaspoon sumac* after the onion. Add small pieces of roasted winter squash, cilantro leaves, and toasted pine nuts to finish. Serve hot or cold as a salad.

Sumac* is a Lebanese lemon-scented spice with a rich earthy color. It goes well with fish, squid, chicken, and lamb, sprinkled over hummus or in pilaf.

pasta with smoky sweet potato & ricotta

This pasta dish has a distinctive smoky flavor as it contains both sweet smoked paprika and smoked cheese.

SERVES 4

1 tablespoon olive oil

1 tablespoon unsalted butter, melted

1 garlic clove, crushed

1 teaspoon sweet smoked paprika

4 cups sweet potato, peeled and cut into 1 inch chunks

3 tablespoons blanched almonds

1 pound **GF** penne or **GF** pasta shells

½ cup whipping cream

½ cup well-flavored **GF** vegetable or **GF** chicken broth (for non-vegetarians)

2 tablespoons lemon thyme leaves, plus extra leaves, to serve

1¼ cups **GF** smoked cheese, grated

1 cup ricotta cheese, drained in a kitchen-paper-lined colander

line a baking sheet with parchment paper.

preheat oven to 400°F.

combine oil, butter, garlic, and paprika in a large mixing bowl. Season with salt and freshly ground black pepper. Add sweet potato and toss to coat.

place sweet potato on a baking sheet and bake for 25–30 minutes or until tender. Add the almonds to the mixing bowl, coating in the remaining oil mixture. You can add the almonds to the baking for the last 5 minutes of cooking time but be sure to keep an eye on them as they brown quickly.

cook pasta in a large saucepan in plenty of boiling salted water until *al dente*. Drain pasta and return it to the saucepan. Cover and set aside briefly.

place cream, broth, and thyme in a small saucepan over high heat and bring to a boil. Reduce heat to medium and cook for several minutes until reduced slightly. Remove from heat and add smoked cheese. Season with salt and freshly ground black pepper. Stir until cheese melts. Pour sauce over pasta, stirring gently to combine.

divide among heated bowls and top with sweet potato and a good dollop of ricotta. Sprinkle with almonds and extra thyme leaves.

SAVORY SECRETS
Substitute winter squash for the sweet potato.

Add broiled or pan-fried **GF** pancetta or **GF** chorizo sausage for a non-vegetarian pasta dish.

Baby English spinach leaves can be incorporated as soon as the pasta is cooked, or served
with the pasta.

red pepper & lentil potpies with feta crumble

The crumble topping adds both texture and flavor to the potpies. They are very nice eaten cold and are good picnic fare.

SERVES 4

feta crumble

2 cups **GF** bread crumbs*

1 tablespoon chopped flat-leaf (Italian) parsley

2 rosemary sprigs, finely chopped

½ cup crumbled Greek feta cheese

2 tablespoons unsalted butter, melted

potpies

1 tablespoon unsalted butter

1 medium red onion, finely chopped

1 large red pepper, deseeded, membrane removed, flesh cut into ½ inch slices

1 garlic clove, crushed

½ quantity prepared **tiny blue-green lentils** (page 109)

½ cup crumbled Greek feta cheese

2 tablespoons roughly chopped flat-leaf (Italian) parsley

3 large eggs

¼ cup whipping cream

line four 1 cup capacity pie tins or ceramic pots with squares of parchment paper measuring 8 x 8 inches. This makes it easy to remove the pies from the tins and keeps the crumble in place.

preheat oven to 350°F.

combine feta crumble ingredients in a bowl, mix well, and reserve.

heat butter in a skillet and sauté onion and capsicum over medium–low heat for about 5 minutes until soft. Add garlic and sauté briefly. Remove from heat and stir in the lentils, feta, and parsley.

spoon lentil mixture into lined pie tins and place on a baking sheet.

whisk eggs and cream together and pour over lentil mixture. Top potpies with feta crumble.

bake for 25–30 minutes until set and crumble is golden. Test with a skewer. If egg mixture is set, the skewer will come out clean.

serving suggestions

Prepare a salad with arugula, grilled eggplant, and/or **slow-roasted tomatoes** (page 168) and black olives. Dress with olive oil and red wine vinegar or vin cotto**.

SAVORY SECRETS

You can make eight smaller potpies in a muffin tray lined with parchment paper. Bake for about 20 minutes.

GF bread crumbs* see **cook's tips—bread** (page 210).

Vin cotto** is an Italian wine vinegar that is available in speciality stores.

SIDE DISHES

salads

apple, mint, & ruby grapefruit salad . . . 128

asian greens & cucumber salad . . . 130

avocado, pear, & Parmesan salad . . . 132

baby spinach & mango salad with lime drizzle . . . 134

baked beetroot, feta, & pistachio salad . . . 136

blood orange, fennel, & olive salad . . . 138

cannellini bean & chorizo salad . . . 140

roasted vegetable salad . . . 142

tomatoes with pomegranate drizzle . . . 144

salsas

guacamole salsa . . . 146

hot & spicy corn & avocado salsa . . . 146

preserved lemon & caper salsa . . . 148

sweet & spicy mango salsa . . . 148

vegetables

baked winter squash with sweet smoked paprika . . . 150

creamy fennel & potato gratin . . . 152

crisp parsnip ribbons or "spaghetti" . . . 154

green beans with hazelnut oil & roasted hazelnuts . . . 156

harissa potatoes . . . 158

lemon & parsley potatoes . . . 161

red onion & fennel confit . . . 162

roasted red pepper . . . 164

roughed-up roasted potatoes . . . 166

slow-roasted tomatoes . . . 168

apple, mint, & ruby grapefruit salad

This is a delightfully refreshing salad. It goes well with fish, chicken, and pork.

SERVES 4

2 ruby red grapefruit

4 cups mixed green salad leaves, including watercress, leaves picked from the stalks

1 sweet apple, such as Lady William or red delicious, thinly sliced (see note)

1 tablespoon small mint or basil leaves

½ cup unsalted pistachio nuts

grapefruit dressing

2 teaspoons red wine vinegar

1 teaspoon **GF** Dijon mustard

1 tablespoon grapefruit juice, squeezed from two reserved rounds*

1 garlic clove, crushed

½ teaspoon sugar or honey

2½ tablespoons olive oil

place grapefruit on a chopping board and use a sharp knife to cut a slice from each end. Cut away the peel working from top to bottom, removing the white pith with the peel. Cut grapefruit into rounds, reserving two for the dressing*

whisk dressing ingredients together in a small bowl and set aside. Thin dressing with a little water if necessary.

place salad leaves in a bowl or on a platter. Arrange grapefruit, apple, and mint over the top and sprinkle with pistachios. Pour dressing over to serve.

note: *Prepare the apple just before serving the salad or squeeze a little lemon juice over to prevent browning.*

SAVORY SECRETS
Substitute blood oranges for the ruby red grapefruit.
Substitute avocado for the apple. Prepare the avocado just before serving the salad.

asian greens & cucumber salad

This salad is simple and delicious. Serve it with fish, chicken, beef, or pork.

SERVES 4

chile lime dressing

1 long red chile, seeded and finely chopped, to taste

1 garlic clove, crushed

1 teaspoon grated fresh ginger

1 tablespoon grated jaggery* or 1 teaspoon light brown sugar

2 teaspoons **GF** fish sauce

1 tablespoon lime juice

1½ tablespoons vegetable or grape seed oil

½ teaspoon sesame oil

salad

2 cups Asian salad greens**

⅓ cup combined cilantro leaves and mint leaves

1 small cucumber, peeled, seeded, and thinly sliced

2–3 scallions, thinly sliced on an angle

3 small red radishes, very thinly sliced (optional)

whisk dressing ingredients together in a small bowl and set aside.

combine salad ingredients in a bowl. Pour dressing over to serve.

SAVORY SECRETS

To vary the recipe, add bean sprouts to the salad.

If it is hardened, microwave jaggery (palm sugar)* for a few seconds on medium heat as this will make grating easier.

Grow your own Asian salad greens**. You can often buy a punnet of seedlings with four varieties including mild tah tsai (tatsoi), peppery red mustard, and Japanese greens mizuna and mibuna. You simply cut as many leaves as required for your salad.

avocado, pear, & Parmesan salad

The flavors and contrasting textures of crisp and creamy ingredients make this salad very delicious.

SERVES 4–6

walnut oil dressing

1 tablespoon verjuice or white wine vinegar

1 teaspoon lemon juice

½ garlic clove, crushed

½ teaspoon sugar

1 teaspoon **GF** Dijon mustard

1 scallion, very finely chopped

2½ tablespoons walnut oil

1 tablespoon grape seed oil

salad

½ cup walnuts

1 lemon, juice only

1–2 avocados (depending on size), sliced

2 or 3 small just-ripe pears, cored and cut into eight wedges

1¾ cups salad leaves, such as baby romaine lettuce, arugula, or baby English spinach, rinsed well and drained

shaved Parmesan cheese, to finish

preheat oven to 350°F.

whisk walnut oil dressing ingredients together with salt and freshly ground black pepper in a small bowl and set aside.

place walnuts on a baking sheet and roast for 10 minutes. Wrap immediately in a clean dish towel and rub to peel off skins. Reserve walnuts and discard skins. Cool walnuts.

squeeze lemon juice over the avocado slices and pear wedges.

place salad leaves in a bowl or on a platter, and arrange avocado, pear, and Parmesan on top. Drizzle with dressing and sprinkle with walnuts.

SAVORY SECRETS
Substitute pecan or toasted pine nuts for the walnuts.
Substitute crumbly feta for the Parmesan.

baby spinach & mango salad with lime drizzle

This salad is the perfect match for **spicy chicken** (page 98), and also goes very well with fish and shrimp.

SERVES 4

lime drizzle

¼ cup **GF** whole-egg mayonnaise*

⅓ cup **GF** Greek-style yogurt

finely grated zest and juice of 1 lime

1 teaspoon **GF** Dijon mustard

salad

2 cups baby English spinach leaves

1–2 firm ripe mangoes, peeled and sliced into ribbons using a vegetable peeler

1 small cucumber, peeled and sliced into ribbons using a vegetable peeler

1 small red onion, thinly sliced

½ cup cilantro leaves (optional)

whisk lime drizzle ingredients together in a small bowl. Add a little water to thin the dressing if necessary. Transfer to a jug and set aside.

place spinach leaves, mango, cucumber, onion, and cilantro, if using, on a platter or individual plates. Pour lime drizzle over to serve.

SAVORY SECRETS

GF whole-egg mayonnaise* is available from supermarkets. Alternatively, prepare **whole-egg mayonnaise** (page 201).

This salad is especially good for a crowd as it can be prepared in advance.

To vary the salad, sprinkle pine nuts or macadamia nuts over to serve.

baked beet, feta, & pistachio salad

This salad can be made several hours in advance and dressed just before serving. Place in the refrigerator until required.

SERVES 6

dressing

finely grated zest and juice of 1 orange

2 tablespoons olive oil

1 garlic clove, crushed

1 teaspoon tarragon vinegar

drizzle of honey, to taste (optional)

salad

2 bunches baby beets or 4 medium beets, trimmed and rinsed well

1½ tablespoons olive oil

juice of 1 orange

2 cups arugula

6 radicchio leaves, torn into pieces

30 green beans, trimmed and cooked in boiling water for 3–4 minutes until just tender

1 cup crumbled feta cheese

⅓ cup unsalted pistachio nuts

preheat oven to 350°F.

whisk dressing ingredients with freshly ground black pepper together in a small bowl and set aside.

place beets on one or two sheets of foil. Drizzle with ½ tablespoon olive oil and wrap securely in the foil. Place on a baking sheet and bake for about 45 minutes or until tender when pierced with a skewer. Cool beets a little. Wearing latex gloves to avoid staining your hands, peel skins and discard. If using medium beets, cut into quarters.

combine orange juice with remaining olive oil and pour over warm beets, allow to marinate for 1 hour or more.

place arugula and radicchio leaves on a platter. Remove beets from marinade and discard marinade. Place beans, beets, and feta over leaves and sprinkle with pistachios. Pour dressing over to serve.

SAVORY SECRET

To vary the recipe, add roasted red onions. Cut onions in quarters, leaving the skin on. Brush onions with olive oil, place on a baking sheet, and bake in the oven with the beets. Remove skin when onions are cooked.

blood orange, fennel, & olive salad

This is a very versatile salad as it goes with poultry, fish, shrimp, or lamb. I sometimes like to serve it on a platter rather than in a bowl.

SERVES 4–6

2 blood oranges

2 small fennel bulbs, shaved

2 cups arugula or other salad leaves

24 Kalamata olives

citrus vinaigrette

1 garlic clove, crushed

1 tablespoon white wine vinegar (or verjuice)

1 tablespoon fresh orange juice

1 teaspoon lime or lemon juice

1 teaspoon **GF** Dijon mustard

½ teaspoon sugar or honey

⅓ cup olive oil (or use half olive oil and half grape seed oil)

place oranges on a chopping board. With a sharp knife cut away the peel, working from top to bottom, removing the pith with the peel. Cut oranges between the membranes into segments.

whisk vinaigrette ingredients with salt and freshly ground black pepper together in a small bowl and set aside. Thin with a little water if necessary.

combine salad ingredients and drizzle with citrus vinaigrette to serve.

SAVORY SECRETS

Substitute other varieties of oranges for the blood oranges.

To shave fennel, use a mandolin or vegetable peeler.

To curl and crisp fennel, place shaved fennel in a bowl of iced water. Leave to soak for about 30 minutes until fennel curls and becomes crisp. Drain and pat dry with kitchen paper or spin in a salad spinner to remove water.

cannellini bean & chorizo salad

I always have canned beans of every variety in my pantry. They are so versatile as they can be eaten warm or cold. With the addition of a few simple ingredients, you can have a meal ready in minutes. This salad is delicious with broiled lamb or chicken and is perfect to take on a picnic.

SERVES 4

1 **GF** chorizo sausage, thinly sliced

14 ounce tin cannellini beans, drained and rinsed

1 green pepper, seeded, membrane removed, flesh diced

1 small red onion, thinly sliced

3 tomatoes, cut into thin wedges

2 tablespoons capers, rinsed well if salted and drained on kitchen paper

24 mixed marinated olives, such as chile olives

2 teaspoons finely chopped rosemary

½ cup flat-leaf (Italian) parsley leaves, plus extra leaves, to finish

dressing

oil from frying chorizo

1 garlic clove, crushed

2 tablespoons olive oil

zest of 1 lemon, finely grated

2 teaspoons red wine vinegar

heat a skillet over medium heat and cook chorizo until lightly browned. Using a slotted spoon, remove chorizo from skillet and drain on kitchen paper. Set aside. Reserve oil in pan.

add garlic and olive oil to chorizo oil remaining in the skillet and cook briefly. Turn off the heat then add lemon zest and vinegar. Season with freshly ground black pepper. Stir well to combine.

place chorizo and remaining salad ingredients in a bowl and gently combine.

pour warm dressing over salad to serve.

SAVORY SECRET
Vary the herbs with whatever you have on hand. Fresh mint and cilantro work well.

roasted vegetable salad

This salad is delicious served warm or cold and is great to take on a picnic.

SERVES 4

¼ cup olive oil

1 garlic clove, crushed

2¼ cups butternut pumpkin (squash), peeled and cut into 1 inch chunks

2 medium fennel bulbs or celeriac, trimmed and cut into quarters

2 medium red onions, cut into quarters (leave the outer skin attached and remove after baking)

2 zucchini, cut on an angle in 1 inch pieces

basil leaves, to finish

olive oil, extra, to drizzle

pomegranate molasses* or balsamic vinegar, to finish

line two baking sheets with parchment paper.

preheat oven to 350°F.

combine oil and garlic in a large bowl. Add the prepared vegetables and toss to coat. Place on baking sheets and season to taste with salt and freshly ground black pepper. Bake for 25 minutes. Remove any cooked vegetables. Turn remaining vegetables and cook for a further 15 minutes or until tender.

place the roasted vegetables on a serving platter and scatter the basil leaves over them. Drizzle salad with extra olive oil and pomegranate molasses just before serving.

SAVORY SECRETS

Pomegranate molasses* is made from pomegranate juice, sugar, and lemon juice. It is a piquant syrupy liquid and is available at speciality gourmet stores or Middle Eastern grocery stores.

Salad may be prepared and refrigerated several hours in advance.

To vary the recipe, add pieces of eggplant to the vegetables and bake as above.

You can also add crumbled feta to the salad and sprinkle with toasted pine nuts to serve.

tomatoes with pomegranate drizzle

Choose tomatoes that are ripe and full of flavor, as they star in this salad. The pomegranate drizzle adds a wonderful sweet-sour taste that complements the tomatoes.

SERVES 4

6 medium tomatoes, sliced

½ cup small mint or basil leaves, rinsed and gently patted dry with kitchen paper

toasted pine nuts, to finish (optional)

pomegranate drizzle

1 tablespoon raspberry vinegar

2 teaspoons pomegranate molasses*

1 teaspoon lemon juice

1 small garlic clove, crushed

⅓ cup olive oil

2 teaspoons chopped mint or basil

whisk drizzle ingredients with freshly ground black pepper together in a small bowl and set aside.

arrange tomatoes on a platter and scatter over mint leaves and pine nuts, if using. Dress with pomegranate drizzle to serve.

SAVORY SECRETS

Pomegranate molasses* is made from pomegranate juice, sugar, and lemon juice. It is a piquant syrupy liquid and is available at speciality gourmet stores and Middle Eastern grocery stores.

Use pomegranate molasses in salad dressings, glazes, and marinades for chicken, quail, pork, or lamb.

Substitute fresh figs for the tomatoes.

To vary the recipe, tear two large buffalo mozzarella in pieces and serve with tomatoes or figs, arugula, pine nuts, and pomegranate drizzle. This makes a delightful summer starter or salad.

guacamole salsa

I love tasting and identifying the ingredients in this salsa, unlike a puréed guacamole.

SERVES 4

2 large firm avocados, diced

3 medium tomatoes, cored, seeded and diced

1 medium celery rib, finely diced

2 scallions, thinly sliced

1 long red or green chile, seeded and very finely chopped, to taste

¼ cup cilantro leaves

finely grated zest of 1–2 limes

juice of 1–2 limes

1–2 garlic cloves, crushed

olive oil, to drizzle

preserved sliced jalapeño peppers*, to finish (optional)

combine avocado, tomato, celery, scallions, chile, and coriander in a large bowl.

combine lime zest, juice, and garlic in a small bowl. Pour over salsa. Drizzle generously with olive oil and top with jalapeño peppers, if using, to serve.

serving suggestions
Serve salsa with **chile beef** (page 102), fish, or chicken. It's also great with anything wrapped in a soft white corn tortilla.

SAVORY SECRET
Preserved sliced jalapeño peppers* are available in jars in the supermarket.

hot & spicy corn & avocado salsa

This salsa goes well with grilled fish, chicken, or pork or broiled beef. I like it spooned over shredded chicken and sour cream and wrapped in a soft white corn tortilla.

SERVES 4

2 ears sweetcorn

1 small red pepper, deseeded, membrane removed, flesh diced

3 scallions, thinly sliced

1 avocado, diced

¼ cup cilantro leaves, or a combination of cilantro and mint

dressing

1 red or green chile, deseeded and finely chopped, to taste

1 garlic clove, crushed

2 tablespoons olive oil

zest of 1 lime, finely grated

1 tablespoon lime juice

1 teaspoon runny honey

½ teaspoon ground cumin

whisk dressing ingredients together in a small bowl and set aside.

hold an ear of corn upright on a chopping board. Use a large sharp knife and cut downwards from the top, as close to the core as possible, to remove the kernels.

blanch corn kernels in boiling water for 30 seconds or until tender. Drain and refresh under cold water.

combine corn with remaining salsa ingredients in a bowl. Pour dressing over salsa to serve.

SAVORY SECRET
To vary the recipe, lightly brush ears of corn with oil and grill for about 15 minutes on medium heat until lightly charred on all sides. Cut corn kernels from the ear and add to salsa.

preserved lemon & caper salsa

This punchy salsa works well with pan-fried or grilled fish, prawns, chicken or lamb.

SERVES 4

1 tablespoon capers, rinsed well if salted and drained on kitchen paper

2 scallions, thinly sliced, or use 6 chives

1 celery rib, finely diced

2 pieces preserved lemon*, pulp discarded, peel rinsed and thinly sliced

½ small cucumber, peeled, seeded and finely diced

12 black olives, pitted and thinly sliced (optional)

1 tablespoon thinly sliced flat-leaf (Italian) parsley

2 teaspoons dry sherry

1 tablespoon lime juice

1 tablespoon olive oil

place all ingredients in a bowl and gently stir to combine.

SAVORY SECRET
Preserved lemons* are available in supermarkets or prepare **preserved lemons** (page 202).

sweet & spicy mango salsa

Serve this salsa with fish, shrimp, or chicken.

SERVES 4–6

1 small red onion, finely chopped

1 small red pepper, seeded, membrane removed, flesh cut into ½ inch dice, or use 1 tomato, diced

1 firm mango, peeled and cut into ½ inch dice

2 teaspoons grated fresh ginger

1 red or green chile, seeded and finely chopped, to taste

1 garlic clove, crushed

2 teaspoons sesame oil

2 teaspoons olive oil

juice of 1 lime

1 tablespoon shredded mint

place all ingredients in a bowl and gently stir to combine.

SAVORY SECRET
Substitute papaya for the mango.

baked winter squash with sweet smoked paprika

This baked squash has a sweet smoky flavor and tastes absolutely delicious.

SERVES 6

3¾ cups butternut squash, peeled and cut into 1 inch chunks

1 tablespoon olive oil

1 tablespoon butter, melted

sweet smoked paprika

line a baking sheet with parchment paper.

preheat oven to 350°F.

place squash in a large bowl, add oil and butter and toss to coat.

transfer squash to the baking sheet and sprinkle all sides with paprika. Season with salt and freshly ground black pepper.

bake for about 30–35 minutes or until golden and tender.

SAVORY SECRET
Substitute sweet potato for the squash.

creamy fennel & potato gratin

SERVES 4

1 cup milk

1 cup whipping cream

1 garlic clove, crushed

2 bay leaves

1 large or 2 small fennel bulbs, very thinly sliced

3 large Desiree potatoes, very thinly sliced

½ cup grated Gruyère or Cheddar cheese

½ cup Gruyère cheese, extra, grated

½ cup **GF** bread crumbs*

1 tablespoon unsalted butter

freshly grated nutmeg, to finish

grease a gratin dish or a square ovenproof dish (approximately 9½ x 9 x 2 inches) and line base with parchment paper.

preheat oven to 350°F.

place milk, cream, garlic, and bay leaves in a saucepan over medium–high heat and bring to a boil. Turn heat off. Season with salt and freshly ground black pepper and leave to infuse.

combine fennel, potato, and cheese in a large bowl and transfer to prepared ovenproof dish.

remove bay leaves from the infused liquid and pour over the fennel and potato mixture.

combine extra Gruyère cheese and bread crumbs and sprinkle over the top. Dot gratin with butter and dust with grated nutmeg.

bake for 1 hour or until cooked. If gratin is browning too much, cover dish loosely with foil. Potatoes should be soft and will absorb the liquid. Allow gratin to stand for 10 minutes before serving.

serving suggestion
This creamy combination of vegetables is perfect served with roasts or alongside a succulent steak topped with **caramelised shallot sauce** (page 199).

SAVORY SECRETS
Use a mandolin or food processor fitted with a slicing blade to finely slice the fennel and potatoes.
GF bread crumbs* see **cook's tips—bread** (page 210).
Substitute celeriac for the fennel. Celeriac has a wonderful earthy flavor and goes perfectly with potatoes in a gratin.

crisp parsnip ribbons or "spaghetti"

Parsnips are such a versatile vegetable. They can be baked, glazed, mashed, and sliced into ribbons or julienne and fried until crisp and golden.

SERVES 4

2–3 medium parsnips

vegetable or bran oil for frying (see note).

sea salt, to serve

peel parsnips, then, using a vegetable peeler, slice into thin ribbons. Alternatively, use a julienne peeler to make "spaghetti". Do not use the bitter woody center of the parsnip.

heat oil in a skillet or saucepan and when hot (but not smoking), fry just one parsnip ribbon or "spaghetti" strand to test the heat of the oil. If it is too hot and the parsnip blackens, remove oil from heat briefly and wait for it to cool down a little. When the oil is ready, fry a small amount of parsnip ribbons, moving them gently around in the oil using tongs. They will take a minute or so to turn pale golden. Do not brown too much.

remove to kitchen paper to drain. Repeat with remaining parsnip ribbons or spaghetti strands. Sprinkle with sea salt to serve.

note: The quantity of oil will depend on the size of your skillet or saucepan, but as a guide pour in 1¼–1½ inches.

SAVORY SECRETS
Parsnip ribbons or "spaghetti" can be prepared up to 2 hours in advance. Once fried and after draining on kitchen paper, place on foil so that they do not soften before serving. Do not reheat. Serve as a vegetable or garnish with puréed potato and/or parsnip or with soup.

green beans with hazelnut oil & roasted hazelnuts

SERVES 4

½ cup hazelnuts*

4 handfuls whole green beans, trimmed

2–3 teaspoons hazelnut oil

sea salt, to serve

preheat oven to 350°F.

place hazelnuts on a baking sheet and roast for about 10 minutes until the skins darken. Wrap nuts in a clean dish towel and rub to remove skins. Discard skins. Roughly chop nuts and reserve.

steam or cook beans uncovered in a saucepan of boiling salted water over high heat for 4–5 minutes until just tender. Drain beans, pat dry with kitchen paper towel and reserve.

add hazelnut oil to the saucepan and warm briefly, then add reserved beans. Season with salt. Turn beans over with tongs to coat with the oil.

place beans on a warm platter and top with hazelnuts. Sprinkle with sea salt to serve.

SAVORY SECRET
You can purchase hazelnuts* already roasted if you wish.

harissa potatoes

I love these potatoes as they absorb the flavors of the stock and harissa. They go well with rosemary and garlic studded lamb, marinated sirloin beef, or broiled chicken with lemon and herbs. They are also great for serving a larger number of guests when entertaining.

SERVES 6

6 large all-purpose potatoes, such as Desiree or Sebago, peeled and cut into large chunks

1 large or 2 medium red onions, cut into eight wedges

2 cups **GF** chicken stock

1 tablespoon **GF** concentrated tomato purée

1 teaspoon harissa paste*, or to taste

sweet smoked paprika

olive oil, for drizzling

roasted red pepper (page 164) (optional), cut into long strips

grated Parmesan cheese (optional)

lightly grease an ovenproof dish, one that will hold the potatoes and onions fairly closely together in a single layer.

preheat oven to 350°F.

place potato and onion in the ovenproof dish.

combine stock, tomato purée, and harissa in a jug. Season with freshly ground black pepper and pour over potato and onion. Sprinkle with paprika and drizzle lightly with oil.

bake for 1–1½ hours or until potato is cooked and most of the liquid has been absorbed.

remove from oven and place pepper, if using, here and there over potato and onion and/or sprinkle with Parmesan. Bake for another 15 minutes.

SAVORY SECRET
Harissa paste* is a traditional accompaniment to Tunisian dishes. It is a vibrant red, hot paste made with chile. It is available in supermarkets and speciality stores.

lemon & parsley potatoes

These potatoes are particularly delicious served with fish. Use new, Coliban, Desiree, Pontiac or Sebago potatoes.

SERVES 4

4–6 medium–large all-purpose potatoes, peeled and cut into 1 inch pieces

1 tablespoon unsalted butter, melted

3 teaspoons olive oil

2 tablespoons finely chopped flat leaf (Italian) parsley

finely grated zest of 1–2 lemons

line a baking sheet with parchment paper.

preheat oven to 350°F.

parboil potatoes in a large saucepan of boiling salted water over high heat for 3 minutes. Drain and pat dry with kitchen paper.

combine butter and oil and brush over potato pieces. Season with salt and freshly ground black pepper. Place on the baking sheet and bake for 20 minutes.

combine parsley and lemon zest. Sprinkle over potatoes and bake for a further 15 minutes or until potatoes are golden and tender.

red onion & fennel confit

This confit is superb with broiled steak, grilled lamb chops, or roast lamb. It is a great accompaniment to cold meats and is especially good with ham in a toasted sandwich. It will keep in the refrigerator for up to a week and can be served warm or cold.

MAKES 1 CUP

1 tablespoon unsalted butter

2 teaspoons olive oil

1 teaspoon fennel seeds

1 medium red onion, thinly sliced

1 small fennel bulb, thinly sliced

1 garlic clove, crushed

⅓ cup balsamic vinegar

2 tablespoons soft brown sugar, firmly packed

1 long red chile, seeded and finely chopped, to taste (optional)

heat butter and oil in a heavy-based skillet over low–medium heat. Add fennel seeds and onion and cook for about 7 minutes or until onion is softened.

add fennel and cook, stirring occasionally, for 3 minutes.

add garlic and cook briefly, then add vinegar, sugar, and chile, if using. Simmer for about 20 minutes or until vegetables soften and liquid becomes syrupy.

roasted red pepper

These roasted red peppers are a favorite of mine as they are so versatile. I use them in many recipes including dips, soups, sauces, side vegetables, and salads.

SERVES 8

8 medium red peppers, rinsed and patted dry with kitchen paper

line a baking sheet with parchment paper.

preheat oven to 400°F.

place peppers on the baking sheet and bake for 30–35 minutes until skins blister and blacken.

transfer peppers to a deep bowl. Cover with plastic wrap and cool.

remove peppers from bowl. Peel and discard skins, membranes, and seeds. Cut in halves or strips.

SAVORY SECRETS

Strain and reserve any liquid from the roasted peppers as it is delicious added to salad dressings, sauces, or soups. The liquid can be frozen.

Serve roasted red peppers as part of an antipasto platter or warm in the microwave as a side vegetable topped with feta cheese and olives.

To freeze roasted red peppers see **cook's tips—peppers** (page 210).

roughed-up roasted potatoes

I really could live on potatoes—it must be the Irish in me! Use Coliban, Desiree, Pontiac, or Sebago potatoes.

SERVES 6

6–8 large all-purpose potatoes, peeled and cut into large even-sized pieces

½ cup olive oil

1 tablespoon chopped herbs, such as thyme and rosemary (optional)

1 garlic clove, crushed

zest of 1–2 lemons, finely grated, or 2 pieces preserved lemon, pulp discarded, peel rinsed and finely chopped

line a baking sheet with parchment paper.

preheat oven to 400°F.

parboil potato in boiling salted water over high heat. Drain well and pat dry with kitchen paper. When potatoes are cool enough to handle, use a fork to roughen the surface.

combine oil, herbs, if using, garlic, and lemon zest.

dip potatoes into oil mixture and then place on the baking sheet. Season with salt and freshly ground black pepper.

bake for 45 minutes or until potatoes are tender, crisp, and golden.

slow-roasted tomatoes

The rich intensity of these tomatoes is superb.

SERVING SIZE

16 ripe roma (plum) or vine-ripened tomatoes (about 4 pounds 8 ounces in total), cut in half and core removed

1–2 garlic cloves, crushed

¼ cup olive oil

2 tablespoons finely chopped rosemary

line two baking sheets with parchment paper.

preheat oven to 325°F.

place cut tomatoes in a large bowl.

whisk the remaining ingredients together with salt and freshly ground black pepper, to taste, and drizzle over the tomatoes. Using your hands, turn the tomatoes to coat.

place tomatoes cut-side up on the baking sheets.

bake for 30 minutes then reduce oven temperature to 235°F and bake for a further 45 minutes.

note: The longer and slower you cook the tomatoes, the more the flavor will develop and intensify. If you have time, you can cook the tomatoes at a lower temperature for a longer period of time.

SAVORY SECRETS

Slow-roasted tomatoes will keep for 3 days in the refrigerator. They also freeze well.

Substitute other herbs for rosemary, for example parsley, basil, oregano, or thyme. Dried herbs work well too. You can also omit the herbs and drizzle the tomatoes with balsamic vinegar before baking.

Serve as part of an antipasto platter.

Spread on **GF** toast or canapés and top with soft goat curd and basil.

Use in salads, especially with mozzarella, Kalamata olives, basil, and a drizzle of olive oil.

SWEET FOOD

cupcakes, butterfly cakes, & fairy cakes . . . 172

dark chocolate budino with cheat's honeycomb ice cream . . . 174

fruit with mint & orange marinade . . . 176

meringues with oranges in star anise syrup . . . 178

parisian macarons . . . 180

potted cream with caramel . . . 182

shortbread sweethearts . . . 184

st clement's jello . . . 186

summer berry puddings . . . 188

upside-down apple or pear cake . . . 190

cupcakes, butterfly cakes & fairy cakes

Who doesn't love a cupcake? Whether for a children's party, afternoon tea, or simply a treat for your family, you are probably going to make these little cakes again and again. They keep well for two days. Undecorated cakes may be frozen.

MAKES 10 CUPCAKES OR
20 MINI CAKES

cupcakes

⅓ cup unsalted butter, softened

½ cup superfine sugar

½ teaspoon vanilla bean paste or natural vanilla extract

2 large eggs

½ cup **GF** self-rising flour*

¼ cup maize cornstarch

⅓ cup white rice flour

1 teaspoon **GF** baking powder

½ teaspoon baking soda

⅓ cup **GF** Greek-style yogurt

2 tablespoons milk (approximately)

frosting

¼ cup unsalted butter, softened

¼ cup cream cheese, at room temperature, cut into cubes

1½ cups pure confectioners' sugar, sifted if lumpy

1 teaspoon lemon juice

¼ teaspoon vanilla bean paste or natural vanilla extract

GF food coloring and **GF** decorations

---

insert paper baking cups into muffin tray/s. Fill any empty muffin holes with water so that the cakes bake evenly.

preheat oven to 350°F.

for the cupcakes

cream butter, sugar, and vanilla in the small bowl of an electric mixer until light and fluffy. Add eggs one at a time, beating well after each addition. Scrape down side of bowl.

sift flours, baking powder, and baking soda together and fold into creamed mixture, alternately with the yogurt. Scrape down the sides of bowl. Stir in milk a little at a time to achieve a soft batter consistency. Fill each paper cup about three-quarters full, then bake for 25 minutes or until lightly golden and cooked through. Test with a skewer. Mini cakes will take about 12 minutes to cook.

cool for 5 minutes before removing to a wire rack. Allow to cool completely before icing and decorating.

for the frosting

place butter, cream cheese, confectioners' sugar, lemon juice, and vanilla in a food processor and blend well. Add food coloring a drop at a time. The frosting can be made while the cakes are baking.

SWEET SECRETS

GF self-rising flour*— use either F. G. Roberts gluten-free self-rising flour **or** Orgran gluten-free self-rising flour. They are available in some supermarkets and health-food stores.

To make **butterfly cakes** bake cupcake recipe as above. Use a fine-pointed knife to cut circles ½ inch in from the edge and about ½ inch down into the cakes. Fill the hole with jam and cream. Cut the cut-out circles of cake in half and position them on top of the cream so they look like butterfly wings. Place jam between the wings for the butterfly's body. Dust with confectioners' sugar.

To make **fairy cakes** bake cupcake recipe as above. Use a fine-pointed knife to cut circles ½ inch in from the edge and about ⅝ inch down into the cakes. Fill the hole with jam or lemon butter and pipe a swirl of sweetened cream on top. Place cut-out cake circles on top of the cream. Dust with pure confectioners' sugar.

dark chocolate budino with cheat's honeycomb ice cream

"Budino" means pudding in Italian. These puddings are delectably rich and ever so simple to prepare. They can be made well in advance too.

SERVES 5 OR 6

cheat's honeycomb ice cream

1 litre **GF** vanilla ice cream*, softened

2 cups crushed **GF** honeycomb**; reserve a little to place on top of ice-cream balls to serve

dark chocolate budino

1⅓ cups dark chocolate pieces***

¾ cup unsalted butter, cubed

3 large eggs

⅓ cup soft brown sugar

1 tablespoon pure maize cornstarch

1 tablespoon unsweetened cocoa powder (I use Dutch cocoa)

additional ingredient

pure confectioners' sugar, to finish

SWEET SECRETS
Bain-marie*—also called a "water bath". This is a baking tin in which the pudding molds are placed and then boiling water is poured into the tin to come halfway up the sides of the molds.

Dark chocolate pieces***— I use Nestlé Plaistowe Couverture Deluxe pieces with 63% cocoa

GF vanilla ice cream* and **GF** honeycomb** are available in supermarkets.

place a baking sheet lined with freezer wrap in the freezer to chill. This is for the ice-cream balls.

grease five 7 fl oz or six ¾ cup ramekins or dariole molds with butter and dust the insides with a combined mixture of 1 tablespoon each unsweetened cocoa powder and pure maize cornstarch. Tip molds upside down and tap over the sink to remove any excess. This helps the pudding to cling to the sides of the molds and to rise.

preheat oven to 315°F.

place ice cream in a stainless steel bowl and stir in honeycomb to combine. Refreeze. When frozen, scoop balls, place on chilled baking sheet, and return to the freezer.

place chocolate and butter in a microwave-safe bowl and microwave on medium for 30-second intervals, stirring each time until mixture is smooth and shiny. Cool slightly. Alternatively, place chocolate and butter in a bowl and set over a saucepan of simmering water. Stir until the mixture melts and becomes smooth and shiny.

beat eggs and brown sugar together with an electric mixer in a small bowl until thick and creamy. Add chocolate and butter mixture and beat to combine. Turn mixer down to a low speed.

combine cornstarch and cocoa in a small bowl and sift over chocolate mixture. Fold in gently. Fill each mold about three-quarters full. Cover puddings loosely with plastic wrap and refrigerate for about 2 hours (or up to 3 days) before cooking. This helps the puddings to maintain their soft center during baking.

place puddings in a bain-marie* and bake for about 35 minutes until slightly risen and tops have a crust. The centers should be soft and runny.

serve puddings either in their molds or turn out onto dessert plates and dust with confectioners' sugar. Serve with cheat's honeycomb ice-cream balls finished with a little reserved crushed honeycomb on top.

fruit with mint & orange marinade

Almost everybody loves fresh fruit salad. It is a refreshing way to finish a meal, especially in the warm summer months. I've added a splash of brandy and the freshness of mint to give this fruit salad a zing. The listed fruit is a guide only. You could use berries only, if you wish.

SERVES 4

1²/₃ cups strawberries, rinsed, shucked and halved

1 kiwi fruit, peeled and chopped

1 orange or mandarin, peeled, pith removed and segmented

1 sweet red apple, cored and sliced

1 cup mixed black and green grapes, cut in half and deseeded

1 banana, peeled and sliced

marinade

1 tablespoon brandy or orange-flavored liqueur, such as Cointreau, Grand Marnier, or Triple Sec

1 tablespoon fresh orange juice

1 tablespoon superfine sugar or runny honey

1 tablespoon baby mint leaves

combine the marinade ingredients in a small bowl and stir well until the sugar has dissolved.

place prepared fruit in a large bowl and pour marinade over. Marinate for about 30 minutes.

serving suggestions

Serve in pretty dessert glasses with **GF** Greek-style yogurt drizzled with runny honey, whipped cream or **GF** ice cream.

meringues with oranges in star anise syrup

Meringue is such a popular dessert that I just have to include it. The oranges cut the sweetness of the meringue and the boozy star anise syrup gives this dessert quite a kick.

MAKES 6–8

oranges in star anise syrup

4 large oranges, for segments

finely shredded zest and juice of 2 oranges

juice of 1 large lemon, strained; you will need a total of ¾ cup combined orange (from above) and lemon juice

½ cup superfine sugar

¼ cup orange-flavored liqueur, such as Cointreau, Grand Marnier or Triple Sec

1 or 2 star anise

meringues

whites of 4 large eggs, at room temperature

¼ teaspoon cream of tartar

1 cup superfine sugar

2 teaspoons pure maize cornstarch

1 teaspoon white wine vinegar

additional ingredient

1¼ cups whipping cream, whipped to soft peaks

line a large baking sheet with parchment paper.

preheat oven to 235°F.

for the oranges in star anise syrup

place an orange on a chopping board and cut a slice from each end with a small sharp knife. Cut away the peel and the pith, working from top to bottom. Segment the oranges between the membranes, place in a bowl and set aside. Repeat with remaining 3 oranges.

place the strained orange juice and lemon juice in a small saucepan over medium–high heat. Add orange zest, sugar, liqueur, and star anise and boil for 10 minutes to reduce to a syrupy consistency. Set aside to cool.

for the meringues

beat egg whites and cream of tartar with an electric mixer until soft peaks form. Add ⅓ cup sugar and beat for 3 minutes. Add remaining sugar, 1 tablespoon at a time, beating well after each addition until sugar has dissolved and meringue is thick and glossy. Sift cornstarch over meringue and add vinegar, folding in gently.

heap 6–8 large dollops of meringue, using two large spoons, onto the baking sheet and draw meringue up into peaks. Alternatively use an icing bag to pipe the meringues. Bake for 1 hour or until dry to the touch. Turn oven off, leaving the meringues in the oven with the door shut for 1 hour as this will help prevent surface cracking.

serve meringues with dollops of whipped cream and orange segments with star anise syrup.

SWEET SECRETS
Rub a little meringue between your thumb and finger. If the texture is grainy, continue beating until the sugar dissolves. You can substitute tangelos for oranges.

To vary the meringue, add citrus zest to the mixture.

If you freeze egg whites, you will require ounces for the recipe above. Thaw egg whites and use at room temperature.

parisian macarons

When I need a reminder of my trips to Paris I whip up a batch of these fabulous almond macarons. Once you've made parisian macarons you will not only want to eat them often, you will possibly make Paris your next holiday destination.

MAKES 48
(24 PAIRED MACARONS)

ganache

1¼ cups **GF** dark chocolate pieces*

⅓ cup whipping cream

chocolate macarons

1½ cups pure confectioners' sugar

2½ tablespoons unsweetened cocoa powder (I use Dutch cocoa)

1¼ cups ground almonds

whites from 3 large eggs, at room temperature

pinch of salt

2 tablespoons superfine sugar

SWEET SECRETS

GF dark chocolate pieces*—I use Nestlé Plaistowe Couverture Deluxe pieces with 63% cocoa. It is available in supermarkets.

Macarons may be frozen filled or unfilled, and stored in an airtight container. I'm usually impatient and eat them straight from the freezer!

line two baking sheets with double layers of parchment paper.

preheat oven to 250°F.

for the ganache

place chocolate and cream in a microwave-safe bowl and microwave on medium for 30-second intervals, stirring each time until mixture is smooth and shiny. Set aside to cool. Alternatively, place chocolate and cream in a bowl and set over a saucepan of simmering water. Stir until the mixture melts and becomes smooth and shiny.

for the chocolate macarons

sift confectioners' sugar and cocoa together then stir in ground almonds to combine. Set aside.

whisk egg whites and salt with an electric mixer until soft peaks form. Add sugar gradually and beat well. Rub a little meringue between thumb and finger. If the texture is grainy, continue beating until sugar has dissolved. Fold combined confectioners' sugar mixture gradually into egg mixture, using the lowest setting on the mixer. It does not matter that the mixture loses volume.

spoon about half of the mixture into an icing bag fitted with a ⅝ inch nozzle. To support the icing bag, rest it in a pitcher while filling. Twist or fold the top of the bag down. Pipe 1¼ inch rounds onto the prepared baking sheets, holding the icing bag about ½ inch above the parchment paper and gently squeezing bag from the top. Lift the icing bag up and away from the macaron. Refill icing bag with remaining mixture and repeat.

hold trays one at a time 12 inches above your work surface and drop them down with a bang. This is to spread the macarons a little. Set aside at room temperature for at least 15 minutes. Bake one tray at a time for about 20 minutes until top is lightly crisp and the center soft. Cool macarons on trays, they will firm a little more as they cool.

pair similar-sized macarons before sandwiching together with ganache. Using a butter knife, spread a small amount of ganache on the flat side of a macaron and place its pair on top.

potted cream with caramel

These little pots are so scrumptious you will not believe just how easy they are to prepare. They are ready in a flash and sit patiently in the refrigerator until you are ready to serve. The brown sugar creates caramel syrup in the base and on top of the potted cream. Yum!

SERVES 6

⅓ cup soft brown sugar

1 cup whipping cream

3 cups **GF** Greek-style yogurt

vanilla bean paste or natural vanilla extract, to taste

sprinkle 1 teaspoon of brown sugar in the base of six 7 fl oz dessert glasses or ramekins.

whisk cream lightly until soft peaks form using an electric mixer or balloon whisk. Fold in yogurt and vanilla. Spoon mixture into glasses or ramekins and sprinkle tops with remaining brown sugar. Cover with plastic wrap and refrigerate. The yogurt and cream mixture will thicken and the sugar will become syrupy.

serving suggestions
Prepare or buy a delicate biscuit to serve with the potted cream. Alternatively, serve with strawberries, poached apples, apricots, or pears.

SWEET SECRETS
This dessert can be prepared up to 4 hours in advance.

Vary the recipe by adding diced banana to the mixture. If you add bananas, you will make 1 or 2 extra desserts depending on how much banana you add.

shortbread sweethearts

Shortbread is generally a Christmas cookie, but why wait until the festive season to enjoy this melt-in-the-mouth treat?

MAKES APPROXIMATELY 36

½ cup unsalted butter, softened

⅛ cup pure icing confectioners' sugar

vanilla bean paste or natural vanilla extract, to taste

heaping ½ cup pure maize cornstarch

½ cup white rice flour

½ cup tapioca flour

superfine sugar, for sprinkling (optional)

pure confectioners' sugar, for dusting

line two baking sheets with parchment paper.

preheat oven to 325°F.

cream butter in a food processor. Add the confectioners' sugar and vanilla and whizz to blend well.

sift flours together and add to processor. Whizz briefly, then pulse (turn off and on in short bursts) until the dough begins to come together.

turn dough onto a sheet of parchment paper and bring together with your hands. Flatten slightly. Cover with a second sheet of parchment paper and use a rolling pin to roll the dough out to approximately ¼ inch thick. Place on a tray and refrigerate for 30 minutes to firm before cutting.

cut out shortbreads with heart-shaped pastry cutters (or other shape of your choice). Place shortbreads on prepared trays, leaving some space between the cookies as they will spread a little. Sprinkle with superfine sugar, if desired.

bake one tray at a time for about 8 minutes or until shortbreads are lightly colored. Transfer to a wire rack to cool. Store in an airtight container.

serve dusted with confectioners' sugar.

SWEET SECRETS
Shortbread will keep in an airtight container for about 1 week.

To vary the recipe, add spice, citrus zest, instant coffee granules, finely chopped nuts, or chocolate chips to the dough.

Drizzle shortbread with melted chocolate for an extra special treat.

st clement's jello

"'Oranges and lemons' say the bells of St Clement's" ... As a child I recall my mother making jello, usually the store-bought kind, for our birthday parties. It was set in orange halves. My recipe is refreshing and has a lot less sugar than store-bought kinds. Even adults will enjoy it, particularly with a dash of liqueur added!

MAKES APPROXIMATELY 3 CUPS

¼ cup warm water

1 tablespoon powdered gelatine

⅓ cup boiling water

½ cup sugar (use less if oranges are very sweet)

4–6 oranges to make 14 fl oz orange juice, strained (remove pulp from orange half-shells and reserve for setting and serving, if desired)

place warm water in a small microwave-safe bowl and sprinkle gelatine over the top. Allow gelatine to soften for 1 minute before placing in microwave. Heat on medium for 40 seconds, stir well, and then microwave for another 15 seconds or until gelatine has dissolved. Stir well. Alternatively follow instructions on the packet to dissolve gelatine.

place boiling water and sugar in a saucepan over medium heat and stir until sugar has dissolved. Alternatively, you can place the boiling water and sugar in a microwave-safe bowl and heat on high for 1–2 minutes until sugar has dissolved.

add dissolved gelatine and orange juice to the sugar syrup and stir well. Pour into jello molds, or set it in a bowl or in orange-shell halves. Place orange shells to rest in the holes of a muffin tray, as this will hold them steady. Place jello in refrigerator to set.

SWEET SECRETS
To vary the recipe, substitute lemon juice for the orange juice and adjust sugar to taste. Prepare jello recipe as above.

For an adult-only jello, reduce the amount of boiling water by 1 tablespoon and add 1 tablespoon of orange-flavored liqueur (such as Cointreau, Grand Marnier, or Triple Sec). Serve with **oranges in star anise syrup** (page 178) or **fruit with mint & orange marinade** (page 176).

summer berry puddings

I like to make individual summer berry puddings as they look quite special when plated.

MAKES 6

18 slices **GF** firm plain bread (I use Country Life Bakery gluten-free bread)

3 cups strawberries, rinsed, shucked and cut into quarters

3 cups fresh or frozen raspberries

3 cups fresh or frozen blueberries

1 cup pure confectioners' sugar

¾ cup boiling water

¾ cup orange-flavored liqueur, such as Cointreau, Grand Marnier, or Triple Sec

3 teaspoons lemon juice

3 teaspoons arrowroot

SWEET SECRETS

If you are short of berry syrup, heat a few more raspberries in sugar and water to produce extra. Strain the berries before using the syrup.

After cutting the **GF** bread into shapes for the puddings, process any offcuts to make bread crumbs. Freeze **GF** bread crumbs to use in other recipes.

line six 7 fl oz pudding molds with freezer or plastic wrap, leaving plenty overhanging the rims.

cut three slices of bread for the base into rounds using a 2¼ inch diameter cutter. Cut each round in half horizontally so that you have six rounds. Set aside.

cut three slices of bread for the tops of the pudding into rounds using a 2¾ inch diameter cutter. Cut each round in half horizontally so that you have six rounds. Set aside.

cut the remaining 12 slices of bread into squares using a square 2½ inch cutter. Cut each square in half horizontally so that you now have 24 squares of bread. Set aside.

combine berries, confectioners' sugar, boiling water, and liqueur in a saucepan. Soak the berries for 30 minutes. Place pan over low heat and simmer for 2 minutes. Add lemon juice. Strain berries and reserve berries and syrup.

dip a round of bread for the base in the syrup and place in each pudding mold. Dip one square of bread at a time in the syrup and line the inside of each mold with four slightly overlapping squares of bread. Fill molds with reserved berries.

strain remaining syrup into a small saucepan and heat gently. Make a paste with arrowroot and 2 tablespoons cool water and stir into syrup. It will thicken slightly. Pour thickened syrup over berries, filling to the top of the molds.

place a round of bread on top of each pudding. Spoon remaining syrup over lid. Fold overhanging freezer or plastic wrap over the puddings to fully enclose.

place puddings on a tray to catch any drips of juice, then place a flat heavy dish on top to press down the puddings. Refrigerate overnight.

unfold freezer or plastic wrap. Turn pudding upside down on a dessert plate. Remove freezer or plastic wrap. Serve with fresh berries or **berry sauce** (page 194).

upside-down pear or apple cake

Serve this cake for dessert or prepare **afternoon teacake**. See "Sweet secrets" below.

MAKES 8–10 GENEROUS PIECES

caramelised pears or apples

¼ cup unsalted butter

¼ cup caster (superfine) sugar

1 pound 12 ounces (about 4 medium) beurre bosc pears or Granny Smith apples, peeled, cored and quartered or sliced

1 tablespoon brandy (optional)

cake

⅓ cup tapioca flour

⅔ cup white rice flour

¼ cup buckwheat flour

⅓ cup pure maize cornstarch

1 teaspoon ground cinnamon

1 teaspoon **GF** baking powder

¼ teaspoon baking soda

1 cup ground almonds

½ cup unsalted butter, softened

⅔ cup superfine sugar

½ teaspoon natural vanilla extract

finely grated zest of 1 lemon

1 tablespoon lemon juice or brandy

3 large eggs

½ cup **GF** Greek-style yogurt

line the base and side of a 9½ inch round cake pan with parchment paper.

preheat oven to 350°F.

melt butter and sugar in a heavy-based skillet over medium–high heat. Add pears or apples and cook for 15 minutes or until they have caramelized, then add brandy and cook briefly. Spread caramelized pears or apples over the base of the cake tin.

sift flours, cinnamon, baking powder, and baking soda together and stir in the ground almonds.

beat butter, sugar, vanilla, and lemon zest in a small bowl with an electric mixer until creamy. Add eggs one at a time, beating well after each addition.

fold in half the sifted ingredients then stir in yogurt and lemon juice. Fold in remaining sifted ingredients and gently combine.

spoon cake batter on top of pears or apples and smooth the top.

bake for 40–45 minutes or until done when tested with a skewer which should come out clean. Stand in pan for 10 minutes, then invert cake onto a serving plate.

serving suggestions
Serve with **caramel sauce** (page 194) (optional), mascarpone cheese, or sweetened whipped cream.

SWEET SECRETS
This cake may be made in advance and reheated in the microwave.

To make **afternoon teacake** omit caramelized fruit and bake cake mixture as above. When cake is cooked, brush top of cake with 1 tablespoon melted butter and sprinkle with a combined mixture of 2 teaspoons superfine sugar and ½ teaspoon ground cinnamon.

SAUCES AND BASICS

berry sauce . . . 194

caramel sauce . . . 194

chocolate glaze . . . 195

passion fruit sauce . . . 195

chicken broth . . . 196

beef broth . . . 197

demi-glaze . . . 198

caramelized shallot sauce . . . 199

easy tomato sauce . . . 200

whole-egg mayonnaise . . . 201

preserved lemons . . . 202

cheesy soft polenta . . . 203

quinoa . . . 204

saffron pilaf with vermicelli . . . 205

fail-proof choux pastry . . . 206

herbed crepes . . . 207

sauces

These sweet sauces can make a gluten-free cake, crepes, or ice cream into a special treat. They appeared in my first cookbook *Sharing Sweet Secrets: Gluten & Wheat free*.

berry sauce

MAKES 1 CUP

2⅓ cups strawberries, rinsed and shucked, or fresh or frozen raspberries, thawed

¼ cup pure confectioners' sugar

2 teaspoons strained lemon juice

place ingredients in a food processor and blend thoroughly until smooth.

press purée through a sieve to remove the berry seeds. Discard seeds. Thin the sauce with a little water if necessary. Store in the refrigerator for up to 2 days.

caramel sauce

MAKES 1 CUP

¼ cup unsalted butter, cubed

½ cup whipping cream

½ cup lightly packed soft brown sugar

place ingredients in a microwave-safe bowl and microwave on medium for 90 seconds. Alternatively place ingredients in a small saucepan over low–medium heat. Stir until the mixture melts.

blend with a hand-held blender or whisk until smooth. Store in the refrigerator for up to 1 week.

chocolate glaze

Use this glaze to top small cakes or choux pastries.

MAKES ½ CUP

3 tablespoons unsalted butter, cubed

½ cup dark chocolate pieces*

combine ingredients in a small microwave-safe bowl and microwave on medium for 30-second intervals, stirring each time, until chocolate is melted. Alternatively, place chocolate and butter in a bowl and set over a saucepan of simmering water. Stir until the mixture melts and becomes smooth and shiny. Store in the refrigerator for up to 1 week.

SWEET SECRET
GF dark chocolate pieces* I use Nestlé Plaistowe Couverture Deluxe pieces with 63% cocoa. it is available in supermarkets.

passion fruit sauce

Serve this sauce over meringues and cream, in trifles or with panna cotta.

MAKES ½ CUP

3 large passion fruit, cut in half and pulp removed and reserved

¼ cup orange juice, strained

2 tablespoons superfine sugar

1 teaspoon arrowroot mixed with 2 teaspoons water

simmer pulp, orange juice, and sugar in a small saucepan over low–medium heat until the sugar is just dissolved. Strain mixture over a bowl. Discard approximately half the seeds. Return juice and remaining seeds to saucepan.

whisk in the arrowroot paste and warm gently, continuing to whisk until sauce thickens slightly. Store in the refrigerator for up to 1 week.

chicken broth

Homemade broth is far superior in flavor and health benefits to any store-bought product. It is cheap and easy to make too. You can prepare this broth one of two ways, depending on whether you want a pale colored or a light brown chicken broth.

MAKES APPROXIMATELY 12 CUPS

2 chicken carcasses or 2 pounds 4 ounces chicken necks

1 large white onion, skin on and chopped

2 medium carrots, unpeeled and chopped

2 medium celery ribs, chopped

1 garlic clove, sliced

10 black peppercorns

2 bay leaves

1 handful herbs—a mixture of parsley, thyme, oregano, and rosemary

place all ingredients in a stockpot. Cover with cold water and bring to a boil over high heat. Immediately reduce heat to low and simmer, uncovered, for 2 hours. Skim and discard any froth that rises to the surface.

cool broth quickly (see **cook's tips—cooling** (page 211)). Remove bones and solids with tongs before straining broth through a fine sieve into a large bowl. Discard bones and solids. Refrigerate broth when cool. Fat will solidify on the surface. Remove fat and discard.

reduce chicken broth by bringing to the boil again over high heat. Partially cover and boil rapidly. Reduce broth by half or more to concentrate the flavor.

SAVORY SECRETS

Chicken broth can be used in sauces, soups, casseroles, risotto, and pilaf.

Freeze broth in containers or zip-lock bags.

To make **light brown chicken broth** place chicken carcasses or necks, 1 brown onion, skin on and chopped, 2 carrots and 2 tomatoes in a roasting tin and drizzle with oil. Bake for about 45 minutes at 350°F until chicken bones brown and vegetables caramelize. Transfer to a large stockpot. Pour about 1 cup water into the roasting tin and stir to scrape up any brown residue from the base. Add this liquid to the stockpot along with celery, garlic, peppercorns, bay leaves, and herbs (as per main recipe). Cover with cold water and follow instructions above.

beef broth

Broth adds flavor and richness to sauces, soups, and casseroles. I like to use some of this broth to make **demi-glaze** (page 198). You can use one large stockpot or two medium-sized stockpots. I find it easier to lift and handle two pots.

MAKES ABOUT 20 CUPS STOCK
OR 8 CUPS REDUCED STOCK

7–9 pounds beef bones

¼ cup vegetable oil

2 medium brown onions, skin on and chopped

2 medium carrots, unpeeled and chopped

2 medium celery ribs, chopped

2 garlic cloves, chopped

1 pound beef sjin (or other stewing steak)

6 ounces **GF** bacon (optional)

4 tablespoons **GF** concentrated tomato purée

3–4 bay leaves

10 black peppercorns

1 very large handful herbs, such as parsley, sage, rosemary, thyme, and oregano, tied in a bundle with cooking twine

SAVORY SECRETS

Freeze broth in containers or zip-lock bags.

For a more intense flavor, add some mushrooms to the stockpot when sautéing the vegetables.

Prepare stocks and demi-glazes the day before your trash is collected so bones are not sitting around in the trash can for days. Or freeze bones and place in trash can just before it is taken away.

preheat oven to 400°F.

place beef bones in a single layer in one or two roasting tins. Bake for 20 minutes. Turn beef bones and bake for a further 20 minutes or until bones are very brown but not burnt. Pour off rendered fat and discard.

heat oil in a stockpot, add onion, carrot, and celery, and cook over medium heat for about 8 minutes stirring often until well caramelized but not too brown. Add garlic and cook briefly. Remove vegetables to a bowl and set aside. Add gravy beef and bacon to pot and brown well. Add 2 cups water to the pot and bring to a boil. Stir and scrape up any brown residue from the base of the pot. (If using two pots, divide the mixture at this point.) Add beef bones, vegetables, tomato purée, bay leaves, peppercorns, and herbs to pot/s.

pour 1 cup water into the roasting tin/s in which the bones were browned, place over medium–high heat, and bring to a boil. Stir and scrape up any brown residue from the base and pour into pot/s. Fill pot/s with cold water and bring to a boil. Reduce heat to low and gently simmer, partially cover, and cook for a minimum of 5 hours. Skim and discard any froth that rises to the surface. This will give you a clear broth.

cool broth quickly (see **cook's tips—cooling** (page 211)). Remove bones with tongs before straining broth through a fine sieve into a large bowl. Discard bones and solids. Refrigerate broth when cool. Fat will solidify on the surface. Remove fat and discard.

reduce broth by bringing to the boil again over high heat. Partially cover and boil rapidly. Reduce broth by half or more to concentrate the flavor. This will take approximately 45 minutes. Cool broth.

broth can be frozen in portions at this point or reduced down further to make a deliciously rich **demi-glaze** (page 198).

demi-glaze

This is a superb sauce to serve with beef or lamb. It elevates a simple steak or rack of lamb to a special meal.

MAKES APPROXIMATELY
20 X 1 TABLESPOON SINGLE SERVES

8 cups reduced **beef stock** (page 197)

2 cups good-quality red wine

½ cup port

place beef stock into a large saucepan or small stockpot over high heat and bring to a boil.

add red wine and port and boil rapidly. Skim and discard any froth that rises to the surface. Reduce liquid to 2 cups demi-glaze.

cool and refrigerate or freeze.

SAVORY SECRETS
You can make a paste with arrowroot and cool water and add it to the demi-glaze to thicken slightly.

Freeze demi-glaze in ice-cube trays. Transfer frozen cubes to zip-lock bags.

caramelised shallot sauce

French shallots are small brown onions and are also known as eschalots. They have a delicate flavor and aroma. Larger French shallots are known as pickling onions.

SERVES 2

2¼ cups French shallots (eschalots)

1 tablespoon unsalted butter

1 garlic clove, crushed

2 tablespoons raspberry vinegar

1 tablespoon balsamic vinegar

¾ cup **GF** chicken or **GF** beef stock

2 teaspoons soft brown sugar

1 teaspoon redcurrant jelly

1 bay leaf

½ teaspoon mixed dried herbs

cover shallots with boiling water and leave for 5 minutes. Drain, then peel once cooled slightly and cut any large shallots in half.

melt butter in a small skillet over medium heat, add shallots, and cook until lightly browned. Add garlic and cook briefly then add remaining ingredients. Season with freshly ground black pepper and bring to a boil. Reduce heat to low and simmer to reduce liquid to a syrupy consistency. This will take about 20 minutes. The shallots should be meltingly soft and caramelized.

serving suggestion
Serve with pan-fried or grill steaks, lamb, or hamburgers.

easy tomato sauce

The quality of tinned tomatoes varies considerably. I use tinned Italian roma (plum) tomatoes.

MAKES APPROXIMATELY 2 CUPS

3 teaspoons olive oil

1 small onion, finely diced

1 garlic clove, crushed

2 bay leaves

14 ounce can chopped tomatoes

2 teaspoons **GF** concentrated tomato purée

1 teaspoon sugar

1 teaspoon balsamic vinegar

heat a skillet over medium heat. Add olive oil and sauté the onion for about 4 minutes or until softened. Add garlic and cook briefly.

add bay leaves, tomato, 1 cup water*, tomato purée, sugar, and vinegar. Season with salt and freshly ground black pepper and bring to a boil. Reduce heat to a rapid simmer and cook sauce for about 25 minutes, stirring occasionally until it thickens.

SAVORY SECRETS
Rinse tomato tin with the water*.

Simply by adding a few ingredients to this sauce you can have a meal ready very quickly. Here are a few suggestions: herbs, anchovies, capers, mozzarella, **GF** chorizo sausage, chicken, seafood, and **GF** meatballs. You can also cook stuffed vegetables such as eggplant, peppers and zucchini in the sauce. It is also great served with **GF** pasta, polenta and **GF** crepes.

To make **tomato mascarpone & basil dip** prepare **easy tomato sauce,** omitting water from the method. Cook sauce for 10 minutes, then add 2 or 3 tablespoons mascarpone cheese and a generous amount of fresh basil or any other herb you have to hand. Transfer to a food processor and whizz briefly so that the dip retains its chunky texture. Serve warm or cold.

Freeze the sauce in portions.

whole-egg mayonnaise

Mayonnaise is very simple to make especially with a food processor. I must admit that I have on occasions resorted to my **cheat's lime mayonnaise** (see "Savory secrets" below).

MAKES ABOUT 1 CUP

1 large egg, at room temperature

⅓ cup light olive oil

⅓ cup grape seed oil or vegetable oil

1 garlic clove, crushed

1 teaspoon **GF** Dijon mustard

2 teaspoons lemon juice

1 teaspoon white wine vinegar

break egg into a food processor and add 1 tablespoon olive oil. Whizz to blend.

place remaining olive oil and grape seed oil in a jug. With processor motor running, drip about a quarter of the combined oil through the feed tube. The mayonnaise will begin to thicken. Now gradually pour the remaining oil through the feed tube in a steady stream. Add a little more oil for a thicker mayonnaise.

add garlic, mustard, lemon juice, and vinegar. Season with salt and freshly ground black pepper and whizz well to combine.

SAVORY SECRETS

Whole-egg mayonnaise will keep for 1 week in the refrigerator in an airtight container.

To thin the mayonnaise, add a little hot water, vinaigrette, or **GF** chicken stock.

Add puréed **roasted red peppers** (page 164) to mayonnaise to serve with shrimp or crayfish.

Add a teaspoon of harissa paste to mayonnaise to serve with **GF** hamburgers.

To make **cheat's lime mayonnaise** purchase **GF** whole-egg mayonnaise, add crushed garlic, **GF** Dijon mustard, and zest and juice of 1 lime. Whisk to blend.

To make **quick dressing for potato salad** combine equal quantities of **GF** mayonnaise and **GF** Greek-style yogurt or sour cream, add chopped scallions, capers and the finely grated zest and juice of 1 lemon.

To make **quick tartare sauce** add 3 tablespoons each chopped capers, pickled cucumbers, and parsley plus 1 finely chopped scallion to 1 cup **GF** whole-egg mayonnaise. Stir to blend.

preserved lemons

If you have a lemon tree it is really worth preserving the fruit in salt. It is quick and easy to do. Preserved lemons enhance so many dishes, from salads and vegetables, fish and chicken, to slow-cooked meaty casseroles. If you are purchasing lemons, try to buy unsprayed, unwaxed organic lemons.

MAKES SIX 11 FL OZ JARS

¼ cups coarse cooking salt

½ cup rock salt (sea salt crystals)

10–12 lemons, rinsed and cut into quarters

6 bay leaves

5 lemons, extra, to yield 1 cup juice

combine salts in a large stainless steel, glass, or plastic bowl.

place 1 tablespoon of combined salt into each of six 11 ounce sterilized jars with lids.

add lemon wedges to the bowl of salt and coat well.

pack salt-crusted lemon wedges into jars, peel-side facing out, and insert a bay leaf into each jar. Press down hard on the wedges to release some of the juice. Spoon all of the remaining salt into the jars, dividing it evenly.

pour in lemon juice to cover. Using a clean cloth dipped in boiling water, wipe around the neck of the jars to remove any salt. Screw jar lid in place.

leave lemons to mature for at least 1 month but preferably 6 weeks before using. Store preserved lemons in a cool place (not in the refrigerator), to mature. Once a jar of preserved lemons is opened, store in the refrigerator.

SAVORY SECRETS

To sterilize jars and lids* place on the hot rinse cycle in the dishwasher.

Shake and invert jars several times during the first week of maturation.

Occasionally a white mold may develop on a piece of lemon that has not been covered with lemon juice. This mold is harmless. Discard mold and continue to use lemons.

Preserved lemons last for more than a year.

To use preserved lemons, discard pulp, rinse the rind, and chop or slice according to recipe.

Generally there is no need to add salt to a recipe if using preserved lemons.

To make **preserved lemon butter** mash 1 tablespoon of rinsed preserved lemon rind with 3 tablespoons unsalted butter and serve with fish or broiled chicken.

cheesy soft polenta

Polenta can have a soft consistency as in this recipe or can be left to firm and then grilled or finished in the oven as in **polenta pizza bites** (page 24).

SERVES 4–6

½ cup coarse polenta

½ oz fine (one-minute) polenta

2 cups milk

2 cups **GF** chicken or **GF** vegetable stock

⅔ cup grated Parmesan cheese

1 cup Fontina cheese, thinly sliced

combine coarse and fine polenta and set aside.

place milk and stock in a large saucepan over high heat and bring to a boil.

pour combined polenta into the liquid in a thin, steady stream. Reduce heat to low–medium and stir continuously with a wooden spoon for 3 minutes.

add cheeses and stir well until they melt into the polenta.

serve polenta as you would mashed potato.

serving suggestion

Serve with **orange marmalade duck ragout** (page 90). Alternatively, you can serve as a starter with **roasted red pepper** (page 164), broiled prosciutto or pancetta, and toasted pine nuts. Weave prosciutto onto metal skewers before broiling to achieve a crinkled effect. Be careful not to burn your fingers when removing prosciutto from hot skewers.

SAVORY SECRET

To vary the recipe, add chopped herbs.

quinoa

Quinoa, pronounced "keenwa", is a superfood with more protein than any other grain. It has a delicious nutty flavor and can be served simply with a squeeze of lemon or jazzed up with other ingredients. Serve quinoa as you would rice.

SERVES 4

1 cup quinoa, rinsed

cook quinoa by absorption method according to directions on the packet. Substitute **GF** chicken broth for water.

SAVORY SECRETS

Add lemon zest or chopped preserved lemon rind, cilantro leaves or parsley, and finely chopped or sliced scallions. Pine nuts or almonds add texture too.

You can purchase natural, red, and black quinoa from supermarkets or health-food stores.

You can cook quinoa in advance. It reheats well in the microwave.

To make **quinoa with chickpeas** add drained and rinsed canned chickpeas to cooked quinoa. Heat through and serve with Moroccan-style recipes.

To make **quinoa tabouleh** combine 2 cups cooked quinoa, 1 cup each diced tomato and cucumber, 4 chopped scallions and 1 cup combined chopped parsley and mint in a large bowl. Season with salt and freshly ground black pepper. For the dressing, whisk 1 crushed garlic clove, 2 tablespoons lemon juice, and 2 tablespoons olive oil together in a small bowl. Mix dressing lightly through the tabouleh.

saffron pilaf with vermicelli

The combination of rice with vermicelli gives a very nice texture to pilaf. You can serve it with fish, seafood, chicken, duck, or lamb. I particularly like it served with lamb that has been rubbed with a blend of Moroccan spices then pan-fried or grilled.

SERVES 4

⅔ cup dried rice vermicelli

3 cups boiling water

1⅓ cups **GF** chicken broth

generous pinch of saffron threads

1 tablespoon olive oil

1 tablespoon unsalted butter

4 scallions or 1 leek, white part only, trimmed, rinsed well and thinly sliced

1 garlic clove, crushed

1 cup basmati rice, rinsed well

½ cup dry white wine

2 makrut (kaffir lime) leaves

place vermicelli in a bowl and cover with boiling water. Leave to soften for 10 minutes while you cook the pilaf. Stir vermicelli occasionally with a fork to separate noodles.

heat broth and saffron in a saucepan over medium heat until simmering.

heat oil and butter in a large heavy-based saucepan (with a tight-fitting lid) over medium heat. Add scallions and garlic and sauté until softened. Add rice and stir for 1 minute, then add wine. Allow wine to boil and cook until it has almost evaporated. Add hot stock and lime leaves and season with salt. Reduce heat to very low and cook, covered, for 14 minutes or until rice is cooked. No peeking until the end of cooking time!

drain vermicelli well and cut through noodles several times with a knife or kitchen scissors. Add to pilaf, stir through, and cover with the lid. Turn heat off and leave for 10 minutes before serving.

SAVORY SECRETS

Prepare pilaf in advance and reheat in a microwave.

If you use a **GF** bouillon cube you may not need to add salt to the pilaf.

You can omit the vermicelli from the pilaf altogether.

To vary the pilaf, add cilantro leaves, raisins or sliced dried apricots, and toasted almonds or pine nuts after the pilaf is cooked.

fail-proof choux pastry

People seem to squirm when it comes to making pastry, especially choux pastry. It really is so easy and versatile too. What could be more delicious than a delicate éclair or profiterole filled with custard and berries? This choux is suitable for sweet and savory fillings.

MAKES APPROXIMATELY 24 X 2 INCH MINI ÉCLAIRS

¼ cup **GF** all-purpose flour*

¼ cup white rice flour

¼ cup unsalted butter, cut into small cubes

2 large eggs

1 egg yolk, extra

fit an icing bag with a ⅝ inch nozzle to pipe éclairs or use two spoons to make puffs.

line two baking sheets with parchment paper.

preheat oven to 400°F.

sift flours together, then sift again.

place ½ cup water and the butter in a small saucepan and boil over high heat until butter melts. Add flour all at once and stir quickly with a wooden spoon to incorporate. Remove from heat and beat vigorously until smooth. It will look gluey. Return saucepan to a very low heat for a few seconds and continue to beat until the paste comes away from the side of the saucepan.

transfer choux batter to a food processor and whizz for 10 seconds. Add eggs one at a time, processing well after each addition. Process choux until it becomes smooth and shiny.

pipe éclairs or spoon walnut-sized portions onto baking sheets.

whisk extra egg yolk with 1 tablespoon water in a small bowl using a fork. Glaze tops of choux with a pastry brush.

bake for 20–25 minutes until puffed, crisp, and golden brown. Place on a wire rack to cool.

SAVORY SECRETS

GF all-purpose flour* I use either F. G. Roberts gluten-free all-purpose flour or Orgran gluten-free all-purpose flour. Both flours are available in some supermarkets and health-food stores.

Mini éclairs are suitable to use for party food nibbles especially **éclairs with smoked salmon & horseradish cream** (page 20).

Prepare fail-proof choux pastry to make **chorizo parsley puffs** (page 16).

herbed crepes

Crepes are so versatile. They can be eaten as a starter, entrée, or dessert (omit herbs for sweet crepes of course!). Try my **herbed crepes with spinach & ricotta** (page 116) or **crepe lasagne** (page 104).

MAKES 8

1 cup **GF** all-purpose flour*

2 large eggs

1¼ cups milk plus a little more to thin batter, if necessary

1½ tablespoons unsalted butter, melted

1 tablespoon chopped flat-leaf (Italian) parsley

unsalted butter, for frying

place flour, eggs, milk, and melted butter in a food processor and whizz to blend until smooth. Add parsley and whizz briefly.

heat a 9½ inch non stick crepe pan over medium high heat and grease lightly with a little of the additional butter. Pour ¼ cup batter into the pan. Tilt and swirl pan to distribute batter evenly over the base.

cook until top of crepe sets and edges begin to turn golden brown. Turn crepe and cook the other side for 30 seconds. Slide crepe from pan onto a wire rack or plate.

add a little more butter to the pan. Whisk batter between making each crepe. Continue to cook crepes until all of the batter is used.

SAVORY SECRETS

GF all-purpose flour* I use either F. G. Roberts gluten-free all-purpose flour or Orgran gluten-free all-purpose flour. Both flours are available in some supermarkets and health-food stores.

Crepes may be made by using a whisk, food processor, or electric mixer.

Crepes may be prepared in advance. They can be layered with freezer wrap and enclosed in foil or zip-lock bags. Before using crepes, allow them to thaw then microwave each crepe for 10 seconds on high heat to make them more pliable.

COOK'S TIPS

bay leaves

These leaves, whether dried or fresh, are used in many recipes. Plant a bay tree (*Laurus nobilis*) in a pot so that you have a constant supply of these aromatic evergreen leaves. They are used to flavor broth, soups, and casseroles and of course are essential in a bouquet garni. To release more flavor from fresh bay leaves, make a tear in the leaves before adding to a dish.

beef, lamb, & pork

Marinate meat before freezing. Thaw in the refrigerator when required.

bread

Freeze a loaf of **GF** bread in portions. Wrap two slices of bread (per portion) in plastic wrap. You can then take the required number of slices from the freezer without having to take the whole loaf out each time.

Save crusts from **GF** bread and when you have about half a dozen, process them in a food processor and store crumbs in a zip-lock bag in the freezer. Alternatively process a whole or half-loaf of day-old bread into crumbs and freeze.

Use **GF** bread crumbs for crumbles; crusts; stuffing for fish, pork, or chicken balls; or coating fish or chicken breasts. There are many desserts in which they are used too. Any recipe that calls for "normal wheaten" bread crumbs can be made with **GF** bread crumbs.

Make **GF** bread crumb stuffing for your Christmas turkey up to a month in advance. Freeze the stuffing so that all you have to do is thaw it in the refrigerator the day before it is required. See **cranberry & pistachio stuffing** (page 96).

If you are crumbing fish or chicken, prepare extra and freeze flat. Wrap well in plastic wrap and seal in containers or zip-lock bags. You can prepare cubed or strips of fish and chicken for finger food this way too.

butter

Cut butter into cubes to have ready for pan-frying. Store cubes in a zip-lock bag.

Prepare **herbed butter** by combining softened butter with finely chopped herbs of your choice. Roll herbed butter into a log shape using parchment paper or freezer wrap. Chill in the refrigerator. Cut into rounds and freeze in zip-lock bags. Serve with fish, poultry, and broiled or grilled meats. You can create many combinations of flavors including anchovy, capers, garlic, preserved lemon, and sun-dried tomato.

casserole & soup

Prepare double quantities of casseroles and soups and freeze in portions.

cheesecloth

Cheesecloth is a fine cotton cloth used for straining broths. If you are unable to purchase muslin, use clean kitchen super wipes.

chicken & duck

Purchase whole chickens and ducks as you will have no wastage. Once you have jointed the bird (see below) use the carcasses for broth. You can freeze the carcasses and when you have two, you can make broth. See **chicken broth** (page 196). Prepare duck broth as you would chicken broth. I like to roast duck carcasses for both flavor and color before making broth. The duck fat will render down after roasting so be sure to pour it off, strain and reserve. Store in an airtight container in the refrigerator. It will keep for months. It is wonderful to use when roasting potatoes. Use duck broth in soups with beans and lentils, in risotto, and when braising meats.

Use poultry shears for jointing raw or roasted chicken, duck, and quail.

To joint chicken and duck, cut down through the skin between the leg and the carcass, bend the leg back and it will pop free from the socket. Cut leg away from the backbone. Repeat the process with the other leg. You can serve this joint as a leg quarter or cut it in two so that you have a thigh and drumstick. If the breasts are to be cooked on the bone, use poultry shears to cut along the breastbone from the neck to the tail. Trim away unwanted sections of the backbone. To prepare boneless chicken breasts, use a sharp knife to separate the breast meat from the bone by following the contours of the breastbone. I like to have the option too of skin on or off the chicken breasts and thighs.

You can marinate chicken and duck portions before freezing. Thaw in the refrigerator when required.

chocolate—to melt

Melt chocolate in the microwave instead of messing around with a double boiler. For approximately 7 ounces couverture chocolate, place chocolate pieces in a microwave-safe bowl and microwave uncovered on medium for 1 minute. Stir and repeat at 30-second intervals until melted.

chopping boards

Use separate chopping boards for sweet and savory foods. This prevents onion and garlic odours from flavoring your sweet food recipes.

Place either a rubber mat, dish towel, or dampened kitchen paper under your chopping board to prevent it from slipping when you chop.

chorizo sausage

Freeze **GF** chorizo sausage to good have on hand as it is very versatile. Slice and pan-fry then add to tomato or pepper sauce and serve with pasta. Use it in pilaf, risotto, soups, and casseroles.

Add pan-fried slices of **GF** chorizo to frittata. A great combination is cooked sliced potato, scallion, roasted pepper, sliced pan-fried **GF** chorizo, Parmesan cheese, and parsley

Add **GF** chorizo and shrimp to pilaf.

cooling

To cool casseroles, soups, and broth quickly, half-fill the kitchen or laundry sink with cold water, add ice cubes and/or ice bricks too if you wish and place casserole, stockpot or saucepan in the water. The water should come about halfway up the side of the container. Refrigerate when cool. Fat will solidify on the surface. Remove and discard fat.

crepes

herbed crepes (page 207) freeze very well. Cook, cool, and freeze crepes between sheets of freezer wrap. Omit herbs and use for dessert with sweet fillings. They are delicious layered with cooked apples and pears or lemon curd to create a crepe "cake" too.

eggplant

Brush slices of eggplant with garlic-flavored olive oil and oven roast or broil until lightly browned and softened. Cool and then flat freeze on a tray. Use freezer wrap to separate the layers of eggplant. Once frozen, place in zip-lock bags or in airtight containers.

garlic

Microwave garlic on high for 15 seconds as this helps the skin to slip off easily. Use a microplane to grate garlic.

herbs & salad leaves

Grow your own herbs and a combination of salad leaves in a garden bed or in pots. Use a pair of scissors to cut stems of herbs. Use kitchen scissors rather than a knife to snip chives before adding to salads or other dishes. Oregano, rosemary, thyme, sage, and bay leaves can be dried successfully.

Add herbs to casseroles and soups towards the end of cooking time as they lose flavor if added too early.

Basil does not like to be kept in the refrigerator. It will last out of the refrigerator for 5–7 days in a jar of water, covered loosely with plastic wrap.

To prevent basil from discoloring when making basil pesto, blanch the leaves ever so quickly, in and out of boiling water. Refresh immediately in cold water then gently dab with kitchen paper to remove excess water before making the pesto.

Basil pesto can be frozen. Cut a piece of freezer wrap measuring about 16 inches in length. Spread pesto on the freezer wrap into a flat rectangle approximately 12 x 6 inches. Fold over excess freezer wrap to totally enclose the pesto. Freeze flat on a tray. When frozen, cut pesto in smaller portions, rewrap, and place in zip-lock bags or an airtight container. I prefer to use zip-lock bags, as containers tend to retain the smell of garlic.

Before spooning pesto over pasta, add a tablespoon or so

of the hot water in which the pasta was cooked to the pesto. This will make the pesto more sauce-like.

jaggery

If your jaggery (palm sugar) hardens, place it in the microwave and warm gently for a few seconds to soften. This makes grating the palm sugar easier.

kitchen timer

It is easy to become distracted once you have put something in the oven or on the stovetop to cook. It is useful to get into the habit of setting a timer so that you do not end up with a burnt offering.

lemons & limes

To extract more juice from lemons and limes, microwave on high for about 15 seconds.

Squeeze the juice from lemons and limes and freeze in ice-cube trays. When cubes are frozen, remove from trays and transfer to zip-lock bags. Freeze the shells of juiced lemons and limes. They will grate easily and can be used for flavoring sweet and savory foods.

makrut (kaffir lime) leaves

Makrut (kaffir lime) leaves have a distinct, sweet fragrance. They are used in Asian cooking, in curries, soups, and also shredded in salads. Keep a bag of lime leaves in the freezer. When cooking rice add several leaves to the water.

microplane

Use for grating Parmesan cheese and garlic, or zesting lemons, limes and oranges. Use a pastry brush to remove grated garlic and zest from the microplane.

microwave oven

I would not be without one! They are such a convenience for thawing frozen food and for reheating food. Remember to allow "standing time" as food will continue to cook. Always use microwave-safe containers. Some types of plastic are not suitable for microwave cooking. To prevent food from spitting, heat in covered containers or use plastic wrap that is microwave safe to cover. Pierce plastic wrap with holes if necessary.

oranges

Freeze whole and use for juice or follow tip as for lemons.

passion fruit

Can be frozen whole, or remove the pulp and freeze in ice-cube trays. When cubes are frozen remove from trays and transfer to zip-lock bags.

peppers

To freeze **roasted red pepper** (page 164), line a flat tray with a sheet of freezer wrap and place roasted capsicum on it in a single layer. Place another sheet of freezer wrap to cover. Freeze then remove from tray and divide into smaller portions. Freeze in an airtight container or zip-lock bag.

plating food

This means to place the food on a plate in such a way that it is appealing to the eye. As the saying goes, "you eat with your eyes". Presentation really is important. The first thing we do is look at the food so color combinations must be visually appealing. Choose different food textures—something crisp with something soft. Keep it simple. I do like to mold rice and rice noodles, soft vegetables and some salads as it gives the appearance of having gone to a little extra effort. Generally speaking, spoon sauces onto the plate and not over the food, but this really depends on the recipe. Wipe around the edges of the plate with a damp cloth so that it is clean and free of finger smudges. Most food looks good on white china although color has its place. When using colored china it should not clash with the food. Always warm plates and bowls when serving hot food.

potatoes

When cooking potatoes for a purée or mashed potato, add one or two bay leaves (remember to remove bay leaves before mashing) or a grated garlic clove to the water to give added flavor to the potatoes.

Alternatively, fold in finely chopped (scallions), fresh

herbs and/or Parmesan cheese. Another healthy idea is to fold cooked lentils into mashed potato.

preserved lemons

I cannot live without them, as my recipes attest. There is nothing mysterious about preserved lemons, yet they impart a unique flavor to so many dishes. They are so simple to preserve yet expensive to buy. If you have a lemon tree preserve your own so that you can enjoy them year round. See **preserved lemons** recipe (page 202).

rice & rice noodles

Cook extra rice and freeze in portions. Add several makrut (kaffir lime) leaves to the water when cooking rice to serve with Asian food. They will give the rice a wonderful aromatic flavor.

Instead of spooning rice or noodles onto plates to serve, place cooked rice or noodles in ramekins or dariole molds. Pat down, so the rice or noodles hold their shape and turn out onto plates.

sauces

Prepare double or triple quantities of **bolognese sauce** (page 105) and **easy tomato sauce** (page 200) and freeze in portions. You can have a meal ready in minutes with a few sauces on hand in the freezer.

skewers

Instead of using bamboo skewers, use firm rosemary stems stripped of all but a few leaves at the top, or use lemon grass stems, which are especially good for fish and shrimp. Cut lemon grass stems in halves lengthways if thick.

spinach

Rinse and remove stems from spinach. Boil water and cook spinach in batches for several minutes. Remove spinach with tongs to a bowl of cold water and cool. Squeeze excess water from spinach. Separate leaves and place on a clean dish towel. Place a second dish towel on top and roll up the spinach. Leave to rest for about 10 minutes. Freeze spinach in layers using freezer wrap. This makes it easy to separate so you can use as much or as little as needed. Thaw spinach and toss in a pan with butter and/or oil and garlic to finish.

tomato purée (concentrated)

Freeze concentrated tomato purée in ice-cube trays and transfer to zip-lock bags when frozen.

washing up

Wash up as you cook so that you are not left with an enormous stack of pots and pans to do later. You want to be able to sit down with a cup of tea, coffee, or a glass of wine and relax once you've prepared your meal, not be doing dishes!

wine

If you happen to have leftover wine, freeze it in ice-cube trays. Thaw cubes and use in cooking.

zip-lock bags

Storing food in zip-lock bags will keep food fresh for longer and save space in the refrigerator and freezer. Use for bread crumbs, herbs, vegetables, and cubed butter, ready for cooking.

Some zip-lock bags are suitable to use in the microwave. Always read labels first before using.

UTENSILS & OTHER COOKING AIDS

A well-equipped kitchen is vital for successful cooking. Good basic equipment is what you need. The simpler the tool the more you will use it. Here is a list of items I have in my kitchen:

parchment paper, foil, and freezer wrap
baking sheets and roasting tins
casserole dishes with fitting lids
chopping boards for sweet and savory food
citrus fruit zester
clear Pyrex measuring jug for liquids
colander
cooking twine
crepe pan (nonstick)
dariole molds
digital scales
egg lifter
electric mixer
food processor
grater
julienne vegetable peeler
icing bag and various nozzles
kitchen scissors
knives, the best you can afford
mandolin
measuring cups and spoons

metal cutters and pvc piping (the kind plumbers use) cut into varying diameters, for example, 2 x 2 inches deep, or 3 x 2 inches deep, used for molding rice, salads, soft vegetables, etc.
microplane, for grating garlic and zesting citrus fruit
mixing bowls of varying sizes, stainless steel and microwave-safe
mortar and pestle
pans—various cake pans, spring-form cake pans, tart tins, muffin trays etc
pastry brushes
potato ricer for making creamy vegetable purées and mashed potatoes
poultry shears
ruler or tape measure for measuring tins
saucepans with fitting lids, heavy-based
scone or cookie cutters
shaker—used for dusting flour on work surface
skillets, nonstick and heavy-based
spatulas
spoons—large metal and slotted, wooden
stick blender
timer
tongs
whisks—large and small
wire racks
wire sieve

INDEX

A

afternoon teacake 191
apple, mint, & ruby grapefruit salad 129
ashed brie & almond oysters 23
Asian greens & cucumber salad 130
Asian rice congee 41
Asian-style omelet with vermicelli & ponzu sauce 52
avocado
    avocado, pear, & Parmesan salad 132
    chile beef with guacamole salsa 103
    guacamole salsa 146
    hot & spicy corn & avocado salsa 146

B

bain-marie 175
basil 211
    basil pesto 211–12
    basil pesto pasta with "no-mess" poached eggs 115
    tomato mascarpone & basil dip 200
bay leaves 210
beans
    cannellini bean & chorizo salad 141
    green beans with hazelnut oil & roasted hazelnuts 156
beef
    beef & mushroom hotpot 100
    beef broth 197
    chile beef with guacamole salsa 103
    demi-glaze 198
    Greek beef kabobs 106
    Italian meatloaf roll with tomato & capsicum sauce 110
beer 7
beer-battered fish & best potato wedges 69
beets
    baked beet, feta, & pistachio salad 137
    roasted beetr dip 18
    simple borscht soup with sour cream & cucumber 49
berry sauce 194
besan 14
beurre blanc 70
biscuits
    Parisian macarons 180
    seeded Parmesan wafers 27
    shortbread sweethearts 185
blood orange, fennel, & olive salad 138
bolognese sauce 105, 213
borscht soup with sour cream & cucumber, simple 49
bread 8, 210
    cumin & Parmesan croutons 43
    flat breads 14
    focaccia 57
    garlic bread fingers 54
bread crumbs 210
broths 8
    beef broth 197
    chicken broth 196
    light brown chicken broth 196
butter 210
butterfly cakes 172

C

cakes
    afternoon teacake 191
    butterfly cakes 172
    cupcakes 172
    fairy cakes 172
    upside-down pear or apple cake 191
cannellini bean & chorizo salad 141
capers
    preserved lemon & caper salsa 149
    sumac fish with preserved lemon & caper salsa 77
caramel
    caramel sauce 194
    caramelized shallot sauce 199
    potted cream with caramel 182
casseroles 210
    beef & mushroom hotpot 100
    chicken in red wine with mushrooms & shallots 79
    chicken tagine with lemon & olives 83
    cooling 211
    slow-cooked lamb with raisins & pine nuts 112
cauliflower soup with cumin & Parmesan croutons 43
cheat's honeycomb ice cream 175
cheat's lime mayonnaise 69
cheese
    ashed brie & almond oysters 23
    cheesy soft polenta 203
    cumin & Parmesan croutons 43
    seeded Parmesan wafers 27
    stuffed black grapes 33
    tomato mascarpone & basil dip 200
    white corn tortilla melts 37
    see also feta; ricotta
chèvre 33
chicken 210–11
    chicken kabobs 106
    chicken poached in ginger broth 80
    chicken in red wine with mushrooms & shallots 79
    chicken broth 196
    chicken tagine with lemon & olives 83
    gremolata-stuffed chicken 87
    icky sticky chicken legs 88
    last-minute chicken 95

prosciutto-wrapped chicken with leek & ricotta 92
spicy chicken 98
Thai chicken patties on cucumber 34
whole chicken with gremolata stuffing 87
chickpeas
chickpea flat bread 14
chunky chickpea & scallion flat bread 14
quinoa with chickpeas 204
seeded chickpea flat bread 14
chiffonade 50
chile beef with guacamole salsa 103
chocolate
chocolate glaze 195
dark chocolate budino with cheat's honeycomb ice cream 175
melting 211
chopping boards 211
chorizo 211
cannellini bean & chorizo salad 141
chorizo parsley puffs 17
Spanish-style omelet with potato, red pepper, & chorizo 62
choux pastry
chorizo parsley puffs 17
éclairs with smoked salmon & horseradish cream 20
fail-proof 206
vegetarian puffs 17
citrus juices 9
celiac disease 7, 10
cooling broth/soup 211
corn
hot & spicy corn & avocado salsa 146
white corn tortilla melts 37
cranberries, dried 97
creamy fennel & potato gratin 153
crepes 211
crepe lasagne 105
herbed crepes 207
herbed crepes with spinach & ricotta 116
crisp parsnip ribbons or "spaghetti" 155
cucumber
Asian greens & cucumber salad 130
simple borscht soup with sour cream & cucumber 49
smoked salmon pinwheels 29
Thai chicken patties on cucumber 34
cumin & Parmesan croutons 43
cupcakes 172

D
demi-glaze 198
desserts
dark chocolate budino with cheat's honeycomb ice cream 175
fruit with mint & orange marinade 177
meringues with oranges in star anise syrup 178
potted cream with caramel 182

St Clement's jelly 186
summer berry puddings 188
dips
quick yogurt dip 18
roasted beet dip 18
spicy sweet potato dip 18
tomato mascarpone & basil dip 200
dressings
beurre blanc 70
cheat's lime mayonnaise 69
horseradish cream 20
quick, for potato salad 201
whole-egg mayonnaise 201
see also sauces
duck 210–11
duck breasts with saffron ginger glaze 84
orange marmalade duck ragout 91

E
éclairs with smoked salmon & horseradish cream 20
eggplant 211
eggs
Asian-style omelet with vermicelli & ponzu sauce 52
basil pesto pasta with "no-mess" poached eggs 115
Spanish-style omelet with potato, red pepper, & chorizo 62

F
fail-proof choux pastry 206
fairy cakes 172
fennel
baked fennel and leek risotto with fish 66
blood orange, fennel, & olive salad 138
creamy fennel & potato gratin 153
red onion & fennel confit 162
feta
baked beet, feta, & pistachio salad 137
red pepper & lentil potpies with feta crumble 124
fish
baked fennel and leek risotto with fish 66
beer-battered fish & best potato wedges 69
crunchy-crusted snapper with beurre blanc 70
polenta, coconut, & lime-coated fish 73
preserved lemon panna cotta with smoked ocean trout 59
sumac fish with preserved lemon & caper salsa 77
see also salmon
flat breads
chickpea 14
chunky chickpea & scallion 14
seeded chickpea 14
flours 7
focaccia 57
fruit with mint & orange marinade 177

G

garlic 211
garlic bread fingers 54
ginger
    chicken poached in ginger broth 80
    duck breasts with saffron ginger glaze 84
    sesame-glazed salmon with pickled ginger rice 74
glazes
    chocolate 195
    saffron ginger 84
gluten intolerance 7
gluten-free food 7
grapes, stuffed black 33
Greek beef or lamb kabobs 106
Greek salad with a twist 106
green beans with hazelnut oil & roasted hazelnuts 156
gremolata-stuffed chicken 87
guacamole salsa 146

H

harrisa paste 103
herbs 9, 211
    herbed butter 210
    herbed crepes 207
    herbed crepes with spinach & ricotta 116
    herby lamb with blue-green lentils 109
horseradish cream 20
hot & spicy corn & avocado salsa 146

I

ice cream, cheat's honeycomb 175
icky sticky chicken legs 88
ingredients 9
Italian meatloaf roll with tomato & pepper sauce 110

J

jaggery 212
juniper berries 91

K

kaffir lime leaves 212
kabobs
    chicken kabobs 106
    Greek beef or lamb kabobs 106
kitchen timer 212

L

labelling code 9
lamb
    Greek lamb kabobs 106
    herby lamb with blue-green lentils 109
    slow-cooked lamb with raisins & pine nuts 112
    slow-cooked lamb shanks 91

leeks
    baked fennel and leek risotto with fish 66
    prosciutto-wrapped chicken with leek & ricotta 92
lemons
    juicing 212
    lemon & parsley potatoes 161
    see also preserved lemons
lentils
    herby lamb with bue-green lentils 109
    red pepper & lentil potpies with feta crumble 124
limes
    baby spinach & mango salad with lime drizzle 135
    juicing 212
    makrut leaves 212
    polenta, coconut, & lime-coated fish 73

M

macarons, Parisian 180
makrut leaves 212
mango
    baby spinach & mango salad with lime drizzle 135
    sweet & spicy mango salsa 149
market mushrooms with garlic bread fingers 54
mayonnaise
    cheat's lime 69
    whole-egg 201
measurements 9
meat, marinating 210
Mediterranean vegetable & ricotta gratin 119
meringues with oranges in star anise syrup 178
microplanes 212
microwave ovens 212
millet pilaf with saffron & green vegetables 120
mushrooms
    beef & mushroom hotpot 100
    chicken in red wine with mushrooms & shallots 79
    market mushrooms with garlic bread fingers 54
cheesecloth 212

N

nigella seeds 27

O

omelets
    Asian-style, with vermicelli & ponzu sauce 52
    Spanish-style, with potato, red pepper, & chorizo 62
onions
    caramelized shallot sauce 199
    chunky chickpea & scallion flat bread 14
    red onion & fennel confit 162
    red onion and fennel confit pizza 57

oranges
    blood orange, fennel, & olive salad 138
    fruit with mint & orange marinade 177
    meringues with oranges in star anise syrup 178
    orange marmalade duck ragout 91
    St Clement's jelly 186
oven temperature 9
oysters
    ashed brie & almond oysters 23
    grilled oysters with spinach & pine nuts 23

P

palm sugar (jaggery) 212
pantry essentials 8
Parisian macarons 180
parsnip, crisp ribbons or "spaghetti" 155
passion fruit sauce 195
pasta
    basil pesto pasta with "no-mess" poached eggs 115
    pasta with smoky sweet potato & ricotta 123
peasant soup 46
peppers
    red pepper & lentil potpies with feta crumble 124
    roasted red pepper 164, 210
    roasted red pepper pizza 57
pizzas
    pizza with a dash of panache 57
    polenta pizza bites 24
plating food 212
polenta
    cheesy soft polenta 203
    polenta, coconut, & lime-coated fish 73
    polenta pizza bites 24
pomegranate molasses 142
ponzu sauce 52
potatoes 212–13
    beer-battered fish & best potato wedges 69
    creamy fennel & potato gratin 153
    harissa potatoes 159
    lemon & parsley potatoes 161
    potato rosti 30
    roughed-up roasted potatoes 166
    Spanish-style omelet with potato, red pepper, & chorizo 62
potted cream with caramel 182
preserved lemons 202, 213
    chicken tagine with lemon & olives 83
    preserved lemon & caper salsa 149
    preserved lemon butter 202
    preserved lemon panna cotta with smoked ocean trout 59
    sumac fish with preserved lemon & caper salsa 77
prosciutto-wrapped chicken with leek & ricotta 92
pumpkin, baked, with sweet smoked paprika 150
puy lentils (tiny blue-green lentils) 109

Q

quail, sage & citrus 95
quinoa 204
    quinoa with chickpeas 204
    quinoa tabouleh 204

R

red pepper & lentil potpies with feta crumble 124
red onion & fennel confit 162
red onion and fennel confit pizza 57
rice 213
    Asian rice congee 41
    baked fennel and leek risotto with fish 66
    pickled ginger rice 74
    saffron pilaf with vermicelli 205
ricotta
    herbed crepes with spinach & ricotta 116
    Mediterranean vegetable & ricotta gratin 119
    pasta with smoky sweet potato & ricotta 123
    prosciutto-wrapped chicken with leek & ricotta 92
    quick cheesy ricotta 105
roughed-up roasted potatoes 166

S

saffron ginger glaze 84
saffron pilaf with vermicelli 205
sage & citrus quail 95
salad leaves 211
salads
    apple, mint, & ruby grapefruit 129
    Asian greens & cucumber 130
    avocado, pear, & Parmesan 132
    baby spinach & mango salad with lime drizzle 135
    baked beet, feta, & pistachio 137
    blood orange, fennel, & olive salad 138
    cannellini bean & chorizo 141
    Greek salad with a twist 106
    quinoa tabouleh 204
    roasted vegetable salad 142
    tomatoes with pomegranate drizzle 144
salmon
    éclairs with smoked salmon & horseradish cream 20
    sesame-glazed salmon with pickled ginger rice 74
    smoked salmon pinwheels 29
    smoked salmon rosti rolls 30
    smoked salmon on toast with wasabi mayonnaise 61
salmonella 9
salsas
    guacamole 146
    hot & spicy corn & avocado 146
    preserved lemon & caper 149
    sweet & spicy mango 149

sauces
    berry sauce 194
    bolognese sauce 105, 213
    caramel sauce 194
    caramelized shallot sauce 199
    easy tomato sauce 200, 213
    passion fruit sauce 195
    quick tartare sauce 201
    tomato & pepper sauce 110
    see also dressings
seafood
    ashed brie & almond oysters 23
    grilled oysters with spinach & pine nuts 23
    sunchoke soup with seared scallops 44
    sumac squid 69
    see also fish; salmon
seeded chickpea flat bread 14
seeded Parmesan wafers 27
sesame-glazed salmon with pickled ginger rice 74
shortbread sweethearts 185
skewers 213
snapper, crunchy crusted, with beurre blanc 70
soup 210
    Asian rice congee 41
    cauliflower, with cumin & Parmesan croutons 43
    cooling 211
    peasant soup 46
    simple borscht, with sour cream & cucumber 49
    summer consommé 50
    sunchoke, with seared scallops 44
Spanish-style omelet with potato, red pepper & chorizo 62
spatchcock with cranberry & pistachio stuffing 97
spicy chicken 98
spicy sweet potato dip 18
spinach 213
    baby spinach & mango salad with lime drizzle 135
    grilled oysters with spinach & pine nuts 23
    herbed crepes with spinach & ricotta 116
    summer consommé 50
St Clement's jelly 186
sumac 14
sumac squid 69
summer berry puddings 188
summer consommé 50
sunchoke soup with seared scallops 44
sweet & spicy mango salsa 149
sweet potato
    pasta with smoky sweet potato & ricotta 123
    spicy sweet potato dip 18

T
tamarind pulp 112
tartare sauce, quick 201
Thai chicken patties on cucumber 34

tomatoes
    easy tomato sauce 200, 213
    slow-roasted tomatoes 169
    tomato & pepper sauce 110
    tomato mascarpone & basil dip 200
    tomato paste 213
    tomatoes with pomegranate drizzle 144

U
upside-down pear or apple cake 191
utensils 215

V
vegetables
    baked pumpkin with sweet smoked paprika 150
    creamy fennel & potato gratin 153
    crisp parsnip ribbons or "spaghetti" 155
    green beans with hazelnut oil & roasted hazelnuts 156
    Mediterranean vegetable & ricotta gratin 119
    millet pilaf with saffron & green vegetables 120
    peasant soup 46
    red onion & fennel confit 162
    roasted vegetable salad 142
    sunchoke soup with seared scallops 44
    see also capsicum; potatoes; tomatoes
vegetarian puffs 17
vin cotto 109, 124

W
wafers, seeded Parmesan 27
wasabi mayonnaise 61
wasabi paste 52
white corn tortilla melts 37
whole-egg mayonnaise 201
wine 213

Y
yogurt dip, quick 18

Z
za'atar 112
zip-lock bags 213

ACKNOWLEDGEMENTS

Writing a cookbook is always a team effort. I would like to express my appreciation to all of the talented people who have contributed to bringing this book together.

First and foremost to Helen Jones who has supported and encouraged me while writing *The Gluten-free Kitchen*. Helen, who is my computer guardian angel, worked with me on my first cookbook, *Sharing Sweet Secrets: Gluten & Wheat Free*. Her enthusiasm, clear judgement, and calm influence are strengths that I value enormously. I look forward to our continuing friendship and many more long lunches together!

Thank you to my foodie friend and neighbour Julia Hendry for her initial edit. Her attention to detail gave consistency to my recipes. I am grateful also to Julia, Meredith, and Wendy for assisting with shopping during the photo shoot.

Many thanks to Kevin, who, like me, enjoys the pleasures of good food and wine. I think it is Kevin's ploy to keep me writing cookbooks so that he eats well every day. The way to his heart is definitely via his stomach!

To family and friends who eat my food and keep on coming back for more, thank you.

Thanks also to Kylie Walker and the team at Murdoch Books. I am so fortunate to have had the opportunity to work once again with photographer Jacqui Way, who together with food stylist Matt Page worked their magic to make my food come alive. The photography is truly amazing and is the result of their passion for excellence. Thank you many times over. I am indebted to Fiona Roberts who at the very last minute was called upon to cook my food for the photo shoot. Fiona's vast experience as a chef and food stylist was invaluable.

You are all my heroes!

METRO BOOKS
New York

An Imprint of Sterling Publishing
387 Park Avenue South
New York, NY 10016

METRO BOOKS and the distinctive Metro Books logo are trademarks of Sterling Publishing Co., Inc.

Text © 2011 Pamela Moriarty
The moral right of the author has been asserted.
Design © 2011 Murdoch Books Pty Limited
Photography © 2011 Jacqui Way

This 2012 edition published by Metro Books by arrangement with Murdoch Books Pty Limited.

Publisher: Kylie Walker
Photographer: Jacqui Way
Stylist: Matt Page
Food Editor: Christine Osmond
Project Editor: Gabriella Sterio
Production: Mike Crowton

ISBN 978-1-4351-3889-6

For information about custom editions, special sales, and premium and corporate purchases, please contact Sterling Special Sales at 800-805-5489 or specialsales@sterlingpublishing.com.

Manufactured in China

2 4 6 8 10 9 7 5 3 1

www.sterlingpublishing.com

IMPORTANT: Those who might be at risk from the effects of salmonella poisoning (the elderly, pregnant women, young children and those suffering from immune deficiency diseases) should consult their doctor with any concerns about eating raw eggs.

OVEN GUIDE: You may find cooking times vary depending on the oven you are using. For fan-forced ovens, as a general rule, set the oven temperature to 35°F lower than indicated in the recipe.